D0908697

ONE SIGNAL
PUBLISHERS

ATRIA

WHISTLES FROM THE GRAVEYARD

MY TIME BEHIND THE CAMERA ON WAR, RAGE,
AND RESTLESS YOUTH IN AFGHANISTAN

MILES LAGOZE

ONE SIGNAL
PUBLISHERS

ATRIA

NEW YORK   LONDON   TORONTO   SYDNEY   NEW DELHI

ONE SIGNAL
PUBLISHERS

ATRIA

An Imprint of Simon & Schuster, Inc.
1230 Avenue of the Americas
New York, NY 10020

First One Signal Publishers/Atria Books hardcover edition November 2023

ONE SIGNAL PUBLISHERS / ATRIA BOOKS and colophon are trademarks of Simon & Schuster, Inc.

For information about special discounts for bulk purchases, please contact Simon & Schuster Special Sales at 1-866-506-1949 or business@simonandschuster.com.

The Simon & Schuster Speakers Bureau can bring authors to your live event. For more information, or to book an event, contact the Simon & Schuster Speakers Bureau at 1-866-248-3049 or visit our website at www.simonspeakers.com.

Interior design by Kyoko Watanabe

Manufactured in the United States of America

1   3   5   7   9   10   8   6   4   2

Library of Congress Cataloging-in-Publication Data
Names: Lagoze, Miles, author.
Title: Whistles from the graveyard : My Time Behind the Camera on War, Rage, and Restless Youth in Afghanistan / Miles Lagoze,
Description: First One Signal Publishers/Atria Books hardcover edition. | New York : One Signal Publishers, 2023. | Includes index.
Identifiers: LCCN 2022047245 (print) | LCCN 2022047246 (ebook) | ISBN 9781668000038 (hardcover) | ISBN 9781668000045 (paperback) | ISBN 9781668000052 (ebook)
Subjects: LCSH: Lagoze, Miles. | Afghan War, 2001–2021—Personal narratives, American. | Soldiers—United States—Biography. | United States. Marine Corps—Military life—History—21st century. | United States. Marine Corps—Biography. | Camera Operators—Afghanistan—Biography. | Lagoze, Miles. Combat Obscura.
Classification: LCC DS371.413 .L34 2023 (print) | LCC DS371.413 (ebook) | DDC 958.104/742—dc23/eng/20221018
LC record available at https://lccn.loc.gov/2022047245

ISBN 978-1-6680-0003-8
ISBN 978-1-6680-0005-2 (ebook)

For Ciara, fat and happy

"This dream you're chasing, the one where you end up at the top of the mountain, all eyes on you, it's the dream you never wake up from."

—MICHAEL WINCOTT AS ANTLERS HOLST
(FROM JORDAN PEELE'S *NOPE*)

CONTENTS

AUTHOR'S NOTE

The following is accurate to the best of my recollection. The fact that I was a cameraman makes it nearly impossible to know what is fully true and what is composite. The camera erases memory by substituting the emotional impetus of the recollection with evidentiary-based voyeurism. It's flat.

USMC RANK STRUCTURE
ENLISTED

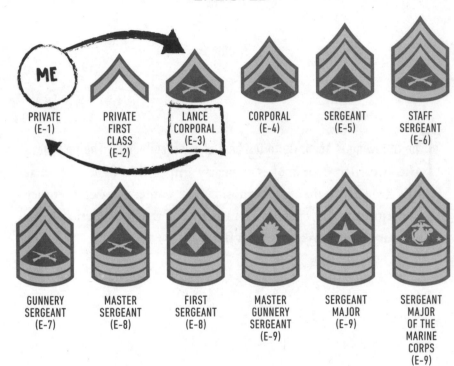

PRIVATE
(E-1)

PRIVATE
FIRST
CLASS
(E-2)

LANCE
CORPORAL
(E-3)

CORPORAL
(E-4)

SERGEANT
(E-5)

STAFF
SERGEANT
(E-6)

GUNNERY
SERGEANT
(E-7)

MASTER
SERGEANT
(E-8)

FIRST
SERGEANT
(E-8)

MASTER
GUNNERY
SERGEANT
(E-9)

SERGEANT
MAJOR
(E-9)

SERGEANT
MAJOR
OF THE
MARINE
CORPS
(E-9)

USMC RANK STRUCTURE
OFFICERS

| WARRANT OFFICER (W-1) | CHIEF WARRANT OFFICER 2 (CWO2) | CHIEF WARRANT OFFICER 3 (CWO3) | CHIEF WARRANT OFFICER 4 (CWO4) | CHIEF WARRANT OFFICER 5 (CWO5) |

| 2NDLT (O-1) | 1STLT (O-2) | CAPTAIN (O-3) | MAJOR (O-4) | LIEUTENANT COLONEL (O-5) | COLONEL (O-6) |

| BRIGADIER GENERAL (O-7) | MAJOR GENERAL (O-8) | LIEUTENANT GENERAL (O-9) | GENERAL (O-10) |

PREFACE

I honestly thought it would be worse than this.

I expected them to come wrap me up in the middle of the night, take me to an undisclosed location, and interrogate me Guantanamo-style, like we used to do with the Afghans. Maybe make me disappear. After all, I'd filmed potential war crimes: detainee abuse, civilians killed without justification other than "the dude was acting shady," recreational drug use by active-duty service members, and Marines using racial slurs as flippantly as the various acronyms we used for everything else. The kind of stuff that went directly against the poster-boy imagery I was tasked with recording as a propaganda stooge for the U.S. Marine Corps.

And I was releasing it to the public.

Granted, by the time *Combat Obscura*—my film composed of footage I'd shot as a Combat Camera in Afghanistan and repurposed into a feature-length documentary—was completed, we'd already been at war for seventeen years, and I'd been in college for four (even though I was still telling people at the time that I'd just gotten out of the Marines). I'd underestimated the level of war fatigue we had as a country.

When I sent a rough cut of the film to the Pentagon to clear it for any classified material, I was met with various cease-and-desist–ish letters from the Corps, head scratching from the Pentagon, and an anxious barrage of calls from the Naval Criminal Investigative Service (NCIS), who were already at work to arrange a meeting with my (ex at the time) wife to talk about the footage. But as far as I could tell, no one had hacked my computer or put me on any of the federal watch lists. My webcam light never turned on unexpectedly and nobody ever showed up to raid my apartment.

Lawyerless and slightly out of my depth at the time, I made the decision to meet with NCIS, not because I was intimidated or scared, but because I felt an obligation to explain some of the moments I'd filmed. These were my friends doing illegal and questionable things in the footage, and I wanted to make sure the Navy or Marine Corps was not going to attempt a retroactive dishonorable discharge for any of them, or, worse, call them back to active duty to then lock them in the brig.

Mentally torn between allegiances and a tepid hangover, I went to their office in Manhattan and was greeted by the awkwardly sympathetic faces of the two agents assigned to my case.

"Now, uh, you understand that you're here on your own accord, right?" said Agent Pascal.

"You have no obligation to speak with us," the other one said. Two White guys who definitely fit the part. One with a DoD-issued buzz cut and overly trimmed goatee, the other with a sort of bland, dumpy-looking dad/cop face. You could just as easily imagine him at his daughter's softball game, or throwing someone up against a wall. I'd seen faces like that on our higher-ups, the lifers who controlled our fate in the Marines, and I didn't trust them because they could turn on you on a dime; go from all fatherly looking and mentorlike to ruining your life by extending your deployment, or kicking you out of the service without benefits.

"But we appreciate you coming down to meet with us ... and uh." He paused for a moment. "Thank you for your service."

I never knew what the fuck people meant when they said that, so I just asked them if I could record the conversation we were about to have.

They both looked at each other and bristled. "See, we'd actually prefer if you didn't."

"You'd *prefer*, or I can't?"

"We would have to table this conversation if you plan on recording it."

Not worth it. I wanted to know what they were looking at in the film just as much as they wanted to know what they were looking at in terms of context and details. *Combat Obscura* was a nonnarrative documentary; footage of Marines giving out soccer balls to Afghan kids was spliced jarringly with other shots of soldiers chasing the same children around with pistols screaming "WHERE'S THE FUCKING TALIBAN?" Cut to a firefight where one of those children gets blown up by a hand grenade he found on the ground and has to be medevaced. Cut to those Marines getting high on post.

It was my attempt to correct the misinformation that had come out of America's longest war by use of blunt-force imagery. *Combat Obscura* was more political statement than story. The film was designed to disturb and upend. You couldn't tell one Marine apart from another in the movie, because I had jumbled it up so much, and now, meeting with NCIS, I could tell they were trying to piece it all back together, and possibly get some names out of me.

They had printed a bunch of still images from the movie and fanned them out on the table in front of us. The first was of a chicken stomped and hacked to death on the floor of a mud hut, surrounded by a circle of Marines' boots. No faces, just the boots; deployment-grade boots with shrapnel-resistant liners, not the lousy ones they issued in garrison.

"What can you tell us about this one?" Agent Pascal asked, pointing to the dead chicken.

I continued to stare at the boots in the photo, thought back to the significance they'd once held: the more time spent in country, the whiter and more faded they got, and the saltier you were considered, as if your old self was fading into a new one. The golden prize of being a combat Marine was getting erased and replaced, losing the soft, untested portions of our stagnant adolescences (youths spent mostly indoors watching porn and war movies) and coming out the other side a confirmed killer, thousand-yard stare and all. People look at me funny when I say trauma has a currency in this country, but for millennials like me (especially the men) who felt lost and identityless, the Forever War offered a direct path to a false concept of manhood. And when you came back, you wouldn't even have to talk about what *really* happened; you could just give people a look and they'd back off. Hell, some of them might even call you a hero.

"It's a dead chicken," I finally said to the agents.

They both chuckled. I couldn't tell if they were trying to be buddy-buddy with me or if they just didn't give a shit.

"We were gonna eat it after we killed it," I said. "It's not like they were just doing it for fun."

They both nodded appreciatively. "Yeah, I mean, I've never deployed or anything, but I can imagine you get pretty sick of eating the same MREs every day. Gotta mix it up sometimes, right?"

"Yeah."

The next image was of a tiny mouse caught in a trap. Its fur was puffed out in frosted tips from the can of air duster I'd filmed a guy use to freeze it to death. Another animal cruelty pic.

"You know there's a dead civilian in the movie, right?" I asked them abruptly.

"We were going to get to that, but there isn't really any way to know if he was a civilian. . . ?"

"He was unarmed, and didn't have a radio or anything," I said. "The locals told us he wasn't Taliban."

"Well, we looked into it and the shot was cleared to take."

Initially I was confused by the fact that they seemed more interested in the images of animals that had been butchered by U.S. Marines than the dead bodies we'd left behind, the families we'd displaced, the houses we'd bombed by mistake. After an hour of them asking me repeatedly, in various ways and to no avail, what camera I'd used to film the material, the names of individuals and commanders who were in charge of them, and so on, I left feeling like I'd been in the principal's office for common mischief, rather than whistle-blowing misconduct within the military. But then I thought through their perspective. Animal cruelty was exactly the type of thing they would want to hide. Civilian casualties were mundane after twenty years of war; they were expected. We'd grown so accustomed to cruelty in this country with everything being filmed, from mass shootings to police killings to the way we point-and-scold the homeless and the sick, that human suffering has become both ubiquitous and strangely disconnected from our full attention, our ability to feel empathy.

The fact that our boys in uniform tortured animals and smoked pot during their downtime in the field revealed the underbelly of the culture, not just of the military, but the country. We were on parade in Afghanistan the same way the vets who stormed the U.S.

Capitol were when they graffitied the walls and took selfies on the floor of the House Chamber.

"You want to know why there's an insurgency in America?" my Marine buddy Dave asks me. "Because we've been fighting one for the past twenty years. You train us and give us the most advanced and lethal killing equipment known to man, send us into a never-ending war, and then you wonder why that shit ends up on your doorstep?"

The Department of Defense investigators I spoke to were not concerned with human death and violence, the obvious result of war, no. They were most concerned with that precious thing we know we can no longer hold on to: American exceptionalism. If our military, our professional warriors, were acting like psychotic thugs—not soldiers who maim and kill our supposed enemies, but incels who fuck with animals for fun—in a foreign country, then what could we really say about our police back home, or the average Joe from Anytown, Alabama? What could we really say about ourselves?

———

For a long time, post-9/11 veterans in this country were given a free pass for a lot of things. It was a compensatory reaction to the way Vietnam vets were treated when they came back from the war. I myself have been guilty of "pulling the vet card" to explain away my shitty behavior to friends, family, the women in my life, the police (when at my lowest). But when January 6th happened and I heard some of the guys from my old unit in Afghanistan were there, it became clear that twenty years of "thank you for your service" and turning a blind eye to what we did in the war was causing more radicalism than complacency. The flip side of the type of misguided patriotism that causes young kids to enlist was now causing those of us who came back to want to tear it all down.

The hyperviolence of our generation of soldiers, the yearning to kill, was not just a product of our training. It was always there in us, that specifically American nihilism that could so easily turn into sadism with the right push. Everything in the military, I now realize, had been either an institutionalized ritual, a macho pissing contest, or a combination of both designed to stoke that sadism; keep it at bay when necessary, enflame it at other times, and then unleash it when the right moment finally came.

Twenty years later the moment has come for us as a nation. A huge part of where we're at in this country in terms of extremism, government distrust, anxiety, and general apathy has to do with our failed wars in the Middle East. When Afghanistan's army finally fell to the Taliban, it was further confirmation that those in power had been lying for two decades about the state of the war, and it was confirmation that we could no longer be called the World's Police. If anything we've been sowing more chaos in the world than preventing it.

When you take the oath to get sworn into the military, you promise to defend the Constitution of the United States against all enemies, both foreign and domestic. For a lot of men and women and their families coming home from our wars, conflicts that had no rhyme or reason, where the enemy was always hidden and the mission was hazy at best, the new enemy is now localized, crystal clear in high definition on our TVs and smartphones. He's seeped into our bloodstream, feeding us like a bunch of dopesick vitriol addicts. Maybe it's always been coming to this, or maybe it's always been this way and we're just now realizing it, but the difference is that now we don't know how to turn it off anymore.

WHISTLES FROM
THE GRAVEYARD

CHAPTER 1

I Am Not Who I Say I Am

When I was sixteen I had two main fears in life. One was going to college and ending up like every other kid in my school, and the other was swallowing my own tongue. I wasn't epileptic or anything. I just didn't trust my mind enough to stop myself from doing it if I thought about it for too long. That was one of my problems. I couldn't stop thinking about certain things, like how content everyone was even though there were two wars going on. Or how people were constantly telling you to "be yourself," but it seemed like all the selves were already taken. Everyone was happily codified into whatever character type from whatever TV sitcom they preferred, and the scariest part was that the sitcoms seemed to be aware of it, too. Everyone was in on the joke but no one seemed to care; it was all dead upon arrival.

I guess you could say I was pretty much a dirtbag. I ridiculed my teachers and did weird shit that made people keep their distance, like putting cigarettes out on my skin. But I wasn't always a piece of shit (I know everyone says that, but it's true); if I remember correctly, I was pretty good when I was little, sort of shy and quiet, athletic; people had to encourage me to speak up more. But at some point I decided to give it all up, and went into a free fall. There's no one to blame but myself for what happened as a result.

One of my best friends' older brother, Waylon, was schizophrenic. Nobody knew it at the time because he was a genius; he'd graduated from high school early and gotten into the University of California, Berkeley, when he was sixteen. He designed computer software that was being looked at by several major companies. But he started to crack during his first year of college and had to come back home to stay with his parents. Everyone thought it was the drugs; he took a lot of mushrooms and smoked too much weed, and maybe there were other things as well. He would go on diatribes about how he could stop time and taste colors, rant about dialectics and things that didn't make a lot of sense, but, being young and innately gripped by all things strange and polemical, his brother Simon and I were infatuated with him. It didn't help that he was better looking than Jesus. High cheekbones and a sunken, lost face, a prettier Charles Manson type with beetle-brown eyes that had an "I got you figured out" kind of twinkle in them, alluring in that way that unstable people can sometimes be.

We would steal my parents' car at night and go joyriding, snort coke in cemeteries, and listen to him wig out. "Let's get silly," he'd say with a weird twerk of his head. Words had different meanings for him, and his body language seemed to be constantly questioning itself, as if he was subverting the underlying foundation of human communication, revealing hidden meanings in everything. A lot of the time I just thought he spoke in the abstract to make what he was saying sound more profound than it really was, but it was still enthralling to hear the shit come out of his mouth, especially when we were fucked up and life seemed to be teetering on the edge of something awesome and terrifying. The fear and the rapture.

At the time I wanted nothing more than to become homeless with him and travel the streets like those jovial bums in *My Own Private Idaho*, minus the whole street-hustling business. For me, Waylon represented a way to escape the numbers, the possibility of breaking out of the confines of human activity that only served as a fulfillment of finite needs. You're hungry so you eat, you're tired so you sleep, you're depressed so you take a pill. Everything seemed so medicalized and prescribed that when Waylon would go days sometimes without eating or sleeping, because he said it made him more conscious of time, I actually believed him. He was capable of going on and on until the road disappeared, and it made you think that there was more to life than just routine, which, to me, was worse than death. I wanted change and new discoveries, and I didn't ever want to get old and sedentary, eating dinner in front of the TV every night like my parents. Sometimes we forget how sad it is to be young, the way we looked at our surroundings and future with such apprehension, fear, disgust, and a pity so deep and full of sorrow that it would leave you sick in bed for days. And love; we had different layers of love.

Then, one day, Waylon disappeared. Nobody knew where. Police were notified but by then he was eighteen and no longer under the guardianship of his parents, so even if they did find him, they wouldn't be able to do anything to make him come back. He became a flyer on telephone poles like a lost dog or cat, those posters you pass by that ask, "Have you seen this man?" accompanied by a grainy black-and-white photo of a guy with a strange smile.

I was left without a role model, and once he was gone, his brother Simon and I grew apart. It seemed that he no longer had any interest in taking things to their limit, which was understandable. He had more skin in the game; the pull of genetics can be a frightening thing. But at the time I saw it as some kind of huge betrayal or act of cowardice. We got into a fight one day in the park by our high school. I was pushing his buttons as far as they would go, telling him he was a pussy and that the reason his brother left was because he wasn't smart enough to understand him. He called me a cuntfuck who was gay for Waylon, and we started throwing down, tussling in the dirt. He was bigger than me, so he got the upper hand and started raining blows down on the back of my head like a bongo drum. I was able to flip around so I was facing him and started laughing like a lunatic. Eventually he spat in my face and got off me.

I wiped the spit off and thought for a moment, then I went after him, delivering a cheap jab to the soft part of his cheek. We squared up and circled each other like in a real fight. Other kids took notice and started gathering around, leering in ecstasy. I tried to play it cool, but I was scared. What was most frightening was how detached I felt. From everything. He must've hit me about twelve times, but I wouldn't let myself go down. I was channeling Waylon. In my head, if I stayed up and continued to get the shit beaten out of me, it would mean I wasn't the fake, insecure little fuck who I really was. I didn't even take another swing at him, just kept moving in close enough so that he could hit me, then I'd back off for a bit and move back in. This went on for quite a while, until my face was deformed and he said fuck it and left.

I sat alone in the park afterward and tried not to cry. At that point I had already alienated everyone close to me: my friends, parents, girls in school who liked me. I had nothing left to gain and nothing to lose, and maybe I had intended it that way in preparation for what I was going to do. So I finished my obligatory high school education while staying with my grandma in New York, attending one of the worst schools in the city, with a graduation rate below 30 percent. I was one of maybe three White kids there, and everyone thought I was a crackhead, but it was pretty ideal for me because all you had to do was show up to class and they'd let you pass.

——

When I went to the Marine recruiter's office on Chambers Street in downtown Manhattan, the sergeant there took one look at my tattered clothes and bloodshot eyes and told me I'd have to take a urinalysis before we could talk. Once it came back clean (somehow, I'm not really sure), he asked if I had a police record. "It's okay if you do, we can work around it. But you have to tell me." I told him I didn't and then he administered the ASVAB (Armed Services Vocational Aptitude Battery) test, an exam that weeded out what he called the "knuckle-draggers, crayon eaters, and schmuckatellis" into the infantry or food service occupational field, and let those with a basic understanding of logic, math, and the English language choose their own destiny.

A sample question from the paragraph comprehension section of the ASVAB:

We always played at all hours; he was a very hyper boy. When I was sick, he would hop into bed and curl up next to me, making sure that I was alright. Riley was compassionate that way, and I could always count on him for a smile. He did not ask for much besides his food dish to be filled and a game of fetch every now and then. He was my best friend, and I loved him very much.

From the text, one can infer that Riley is:

A. A good secret keeper
B. The author's distant cousin
C. Really mean
D. The family dog

After I scored high enough, the sergeant asked me what I wanted to be. I had apparently done more research than the average dipshit he was used to, and told him I was interested in Combat Camera. He looked at me like I'd just pissed in his corn flakes.

"Oh," he said, "you're one of *those* kids."

CHAPTER 2

Laughter (or) Mirth

They took us to the place where they do the thing that makes you a Marine, and it was like being in a shitty airport for too long. No sleep till the red-eye, except the red-eye wasn't coming. Also, no places to lie down. I'd never been homeless but I felt that would be infinitely better than what was happening now. If I were homeless, sprawled out in Times Square, I could think about celebrities. I could imagine rolling around in plush white hotel sheets while slurping down fruit cocktails and munching benzos, and how great that would be. But here thinking about the good life I'd never see felt even more punishing.

There's a hulking, ogre-like creature in front of me who seems like he knows what's going on. He's got his ass so puckered up into his pelvis that it looks like it might burst out the other side. I tap him on the shoulder and ask him when we can sleep. He shushes me like a Nazi, and suddenly I realize that some of these guys are really prepared for this. They must have watched videos online or been in one of those high school ROTC programs, gotten the low-

down from recruiters. I can't believe that no one has prepared me.
I feel like I should say something to someone but I can't tell if it's
started already.

The civilians who work on the base throw a bunch of stuff at us
that we load into the mesh laundry bags we have. I say thank you.
They tell me to shut the fuck up, which hurts worse than a punch
to the gut, the realization that even the civilians were told to treat
us like dogs.

I tap the puckered asshole in front of me on the shoulder again.
He says, "What's up, man?" which I appreciate. He's not a total Nazi.

I say, "What the hell is going on? I just got off a four-hour
flight. I'm pretty sure it's like four a.m. right now. When are we
going to get to go to sleep?"

"Dude," he says, "I don't know. I was on the same flight as you."

"Word," I say.

"What?" he says.

"Yeah, okay."

The southern air is stagnant and feels like you're drowning in
redneck breath. They made this heat for the swamp rats, not for
you, you think. But then you realize that no one ever liked you, and
that perhaps this is your punishment, and that you should probably
cry for being the way you are. It would be good to cry. But if you
did, the puckered asshole in front of you would probably be all
weird about it. He seems like a good kid and you don't want to put
that burden on him.

After they finish throwing random shit into our mesh laundry bags, someone gives me an M16 and reads off the number
located on the buttstock. It's probably 6 a.m. by then and the sun
is coming out upside down, and I don't know what is happening
and I can't believe I've just been handed a rifle. I prop it over my
shoulder like a drunken hillbilly and the Marine who handed it to

me grabs me like a cow, tells me to hold it out six inches in front of me.

There're other guys now, all sitting in the grass. Homesickness, anywhere-but-here-sickness, it comes on strong in the early dawn of bad decisions. But I jerk my mind into focus, and I go over to the ass pucker, who is now sitting Indian-style in the grass staring at his rifle as if it's some kind of gift from God. I plop down next to him and say, "What the fuck? I didn't think they'd give us rifles on the first day."

He frowns like I'm an absolute idiot and continues staring at his gun, and I realize that I hate him and probably never want to talk to him again.

Eventually we all get up and get marched over to this place they call the "squad bay," which basically looks like some kind of detention center. Everything smells inhuman—dirty mop buckets and cheap metal.

The drill instructors (DIs) don't enunciate, they shriek, and you can tell that most of them are losing their voices, but they're pushing through the pain. It hurts to hear them.

For some reason, they start a lot of sentences with "Hello!"

"Hello, running!" one of them says to this sloth-like Black kid with wide-frame BCG glasses hanging off his face. He can barely carry his shit into the squad bay—gear spilling out everywhere—which I find absolutely hilarious. My mesh is still in good mesh. I'm glad I've got my shit together, at least a little better than him. A lot of these kids are from the South and I can't believe how lethargic they are. This instills confidence in my physical capabilities.

But the feeling soon vanishes when one of the DIs comes over to me and looks at my name tag: LAGOZE. A fake name, a nothing name, an Ellis Island variation.

"Whuh?" he huffs. "La-faggot?"

"Aye, sir," I croak. This response puzzles him, as I've acknowledged that I understand what he said, but haven't confirmed whether it is the correct pronunciation.

There are a few DIs running around like cracked-out pit bulls. I catch one of them in my periphery; he's screaming like we're in a horror movie. Maybe he's not wrong. Sergeant Eamon. The man is an action figure; his torso is a keg and his arms are branches. He likes raising them when he screams, as if he's summoning a demon out of hell. This deeply concerns me, mostly because I know it is a performance, and to perform that well you have to believe it somewhat.

They start throwing all the shit in our mesh laundry bags everywhere; boots, soap, envelopes for writing home, scuzz brushes, socks, skivvies, ponchos, toothbrushes. Everything gets mixed up, which is kind of irritating because we're still not fully aware of what's happening.

We look like bags of asses, the DIs tell us.

Eventually a beautiful, short Latino man with perfect sleeves rolled up to his biceps comes out and tells the other DIs to chill. He's immaculate; a silky bronze tan and a face chiseled from combat. He tells us he's our senior drill instructor, Gunnery Sergeant Soto, but I'm not listening, just staring at his sleeves and glad the other ones have stopped throwing our shit everywhere. We sit down cross-legged, Indian-style, but then stand up again because we didn't all do it at the same time. After the seventh try, we nail it.

Sergeant Eamon is disappointed, and I think he keeps eyeing me. The man is absolutely a problem, because he takes his role very seriously, and I don't know what my role is yet. If this is all real, then it might be best to jump in. The threat of death seems legitimate because I'm only eighteen and have been lounging most of my life. But there's also a part of me that suspects I can make it through detached, so my gut struggles to find a middle ground somewhere between the blood-red asphalt that lines the floor and the lazy sunlight coming from outside.

After a short spiel from our senior DI laying out the rules of what they can and can't do to us, most of which they've already broken, he calls us back to attention so the others can berate us some more. Eamon rips apart a metal bunk bed and throws half of it into the center of the squad bay. Then he starts screaming incoherently in a kid's face. Recruits run amid the melee trying to put the bunk bed back together but are stiff-armed by the DIs whenever they get too close to them. We are to stay at least arm's length away from them at all times because we are disgusting things.

———

I'm afraid I'll have a panic attack, like I used to have in high school when I thought about my future. Now there is definitely the potential for a panic attack because my future is this, for four years, and we've been standing at attention for several hours, and I've been stuck in one position for too long and I start to think about swallowing my tongue. To repeat, I'm not epileptic; I just feel like I have the capacity to do it if I think about it for too long. My knees are buckling and I'm quietly praying to a god I don't believe in. Eamon is watching, a cutthroat smile peeking out from under his Smokey Bear.

Before he can get to me, however, an Asian kid across from me makes a beeline for the door. He crashes it open with the force of a thousand men and flings himself headfirst off the balcony with a resigned sort of whimper. Everyone stops. The DIs run out of the squad bay.

The kid is on the ground outside crying. I think he was trying to kill himself but we're on the first floor so maybe he was just trying to give the impression that he was trying to kill himself so he could go home. Home felt like a good place to be.

When Sergeant Eamon gets outside, he lets out a triumphant yet mournful wail that shakes the trees and reverberates through the squad bay. "CHAAAAANG!!" he bellows.

The kid's name is Guo. He has a terrible lisp and I wish for his sake he didn't. I'm worried about him because he seems like the type who actually thought this was going to be like the commercials.

We keep him on suicide watch for a few nights, which means we have to shine our "moonbeams" (flashlights) with blue filters on his face as he sleeps. It's like a weird vigil. The third night we have him on suicide watch with our blue lights, Berry, a kid with a head the size of a literal watermelon, tries to hang himself by tying his belt through one of the vents in the bathroom. But he breaks the vent. So then we have two kids on suicide watch with blue lights.

Our senior DI confronts us about this during one of his talks. "Is it that bad?" he asks us. Some of us recruits shake our heads vigorously. "No!" we scream with our eyes. If anything, it could be harder. Our senior DI doesn't care. He tells us that we'll just have to keep better accountability of each other. In DI-speak this means that we should beat the shit out of Guo and Berry, which we do. But once that happens, it opens the floodgates and everybody starts beating the shit out of everybody for no reason. There's a fight every other day over petty things, as we begin to police each other. It feels like prison but, apparently, we're being trained to go to war. The DIs are pleased by this, as it means their job is being done for them.

During drill one day, while we're being forced to march around in circles over and over until our limbs get squirrelly and everybody's bumping into each other like a sweaty, human slinky, Machado, whom Sergeant Eamon calls "Dorito" (they're very clever with the names: they call this other kid, Puglisi, "Pug Ugly Please Me"), punches me in the arm because I'm not screaming loud enough.

"C'mon, dude, scream!" he cries.

I wait till we get back into the squad bay, out of the oppressive swamp heat, and hit him back, as hard as I physically can. He goes flying and trips over his foot locker, almost clipping his head on his rack. It feels really good, but somehow, I pinched my pinky nail on his tooth or something when I hit him, and within a few days it's turning black.

While we're waiting to enter the chow hall one morning, Eamon comes over to me and slowly peels the dead nail off my finger.

"Scream," he says, almost sympathetically.

"Aye, sir," I scream.

"SCREAM," he says again, but this time his breakfast comes flying out of his mouth into my eyes. It smells like curdled milk. I scream again, but this time I do it so loud that I start to cry and piss myself a little. He's satisfied and begins to walk away, and as he does, I mouth the word "motherfucker." Just as I'm getting to the "er" part he turns and looks back at me. His eyes light up as I see the war crimes flash upon his brow. I suspect that he may have thought I was calling him the N-word. There're a lot of racist kids in the platoon, so it wouldn't be out of the ordinary.

I give him a look like, no, I'm from New York, but he follows me into the chow hall and makes me get a bunch of hard-boiled eggs, white bread, a box of raisins, some mustard and mayo, and a bottle of Powerade. Then he takes me outside and has me mash it all into the bottle of Powerade and chug it, as he counts down from thirty. Then he I-T's me, Incentive Training, and makes me do a bunch of push-ups and sit-ups and burpees until, he hopes, I puke it all up. But this so happens to be one of my greatest talents, not puking. Years of ingesting large quantities of alcohol and narcotics have made me puke-resistant. I'm a dry heaver. I'll gag occasionally, but my stomach will never produce anything. And so I deny Eamon the pleasure.

Eventually he stops and says, "Oh, you think you're hard, don't you?"

Not anymore, but I definitely used to. I plead, "No, sir." He doesn't believe me. He tells me I'm gonna be his bitch the rest of the time he's got me. My throat hurts.

The next week we go out to shoot our M16s for the first time. It's 3 a.m. and the stars are shining so big they look like they might come crashing down.

"It's so fucking beautiful, isn't it, Lagoze," one of the DIs says in mock-stoner voice, when he catches me gazing at the sky.

"No, sir."

When we get to the range, Sergeant Eamon makes Guo run laps around it while screaming, "Me so horny!" over and over again, which the rest of the crew finds hilarious, until he starts losing his voice and is sort of half sobbing and out of breath. Some of us keep giggling nonetheless. Everything is funny and everything is awful. "Me tho hawny! Me tho hawny!" he brays through his lisp, until he's on the verge of passing out and someone makes him stop.

When it turns out Guo is a terrible shot and misses every target that's presented to him, despite the instructors trying their best to help him, Eamon gets fed up and bends Guo's trigger finger back until it breaks. He says it's an accident. I'm relieved because Guo finally gets to go home, and Sergeant Eamon gets busted down to corporal and moved to another platoon.

Each Wednesday they put us in a big white room and give us PowerPoint presentations about Marine Corps history and how to see best in the dark and different adrenaline levels you experience when you get shot at, labeled by color. Blue is too calm, it's like you don't give a fuck what's happening; red is too freaked out and you become useless—you could get tunnel vision or freeze up. The sweet spot is green, where you're scared but still in control. The PowerPoint guy says he'll give us a treat and shows us a bunch of "moto" (short for motivational) videos of combat from Iraq, with Avenged Sevenfold or some other shitty band playing in the background. Guys running around in Fallujah blowing stuff up and clearing houses. We're promised this will be us soon; no longer kids, but men with real bullets in our weapons, pink-misting real "grapes" and leaving real destroyed cities in our wake. Marines flashing peace signs next to bloated corpses left lying in the street. Tanks shooting at mosques, chipping holes in the sides piece by piece. We eighteen-year-old washouts find this intoxicating. When you've been fed a steady diet of kill-centrism, gearing you up at the same time as they break you down, these videos are affirmation that you might get to be in it soon, a member of the thousand-yard-stare club. Trauma is a currency for American boys looking to define themselves.

I wonder if this was shot by Combat Camera. If so, it will eventually be me recording. I feel my adrenal gland drip acid into my intestines, the dank ambience of shit and war emanating off the screen. There is something horrifying yet beautiful about the footage, a collage of close encounters with mortality, pain, cadavers, all set to the backdrop of American fuck-you. But it's the intimacy most of all that encroaches, the knowledge that the person filming is a Marine with a gun.

The PowerPoint man gets serious and says he's going to show us another video. "Hey, devils, listen up," he says. "This is what happens when you leave a Marine behind." He clicks a button and on comes grainy footage of an American prisoner with dead eyes staring blankly ahead. Judging from the looks of him, he is too sleep-deprived to know what's happening. The usual hooded men with their machetes and AKs stand behind him getting ready.

"Eyes, bitches," the DIs say in voices like roadkill. "*Eyes.*"

"Open, sir," we respond.

"Okay . . . *EYES.*"

"OPEN, SIR!"

They want to make sure we're not sleeping for this.

The PowerPoint guy plays the video. The hooded dudes grab the POW's head and yank it back, and suddenly his dead eyes come alive in pixelated terror. He starts screaming, then the screaming turns into a kind of guttural animal droning as the blade cuts in, the realization setting in, and the droning lasts awhile before the gurgling, until there is nothing and the head is floating, eyes still open, staring past the camera.

My bunkmate, Matty Burgos, is so good-looking that the DIs make fun of him and insist he become part of the Silent Drill Team, where you travel around parading in your dress blues, throwing rifles at each other for recruiting commercials. Matty leans over to me and whispers that he's already seen that beheading video and thinks that it's fake.

"What do you mean, fake?" I ask.

"Like, photoshopped or something, by the hajis," he says. "For propaganda, you know?"

They hear us and make us do push-ups and sit-ups in one of the sand pits outside until Matty pukes. Eamon appears out of nowhere behind him and begins rubbing his face in it while wailing his usual mournful song that radiates horror and glee, a tacit acknowledgment that what he is doing is sick and cruel, but that is the way it is going to be with Eamon, busted-down rank or not.

In the beginning there was a sense that we were a different entity from the DIs, that our young spunk would carry us through together, collectively. But it became clear quite early on that boot camp is not an adventure, and it is not transcendent. It is bleak and tiresome, and makes your worst traits materialize shamelessly. And because we all hated each other after a certain point, with our stupid shaved heads and dank, disgusting bodies—we began to fall deeply in love with our DIs. They became the hot girls we could never attain in high school, with their tattoos and steroids and Monster energy drinks, the overwhelming scent of Old Spice Body Wash that would waft through the air as they passed by us down the line like fascist sharks.

"Y'all smell that? Fuckin' fish market out here," Staff Sergeant Hert would say whenever we marched past the female side of the base.

"Aye, sir!" we'd all cheer, and giggle to each other, walking with our rifles six inches out from our chests in little columns like ugly ducklings who hadn't slept or washed or changed clothes in days, the stench of beaten-dog obedience and Stockholm syndrome radiating off our grime-streaked, acne-ridden faces. Outbursts of misogyny, revealing flashes wrapped in seductive tidbits of wry and savage humor, passed for niceties out there. Short moments when we weren't being yelled at. Those times made us the happiest campers.

After a while we even began to miss Sergeant Eamon, Corporal Eamon now, and wondered what kind of hell he was putting his new platoon through.

"Remember when he said he'd rip Berry's head off and roll it down the squad bay like a bowling ball?" we reminisced.

"Such a badass."

By the end guys were hoping to get I-T'd so they could get some quality alone time with the DIs. They, of course, caught on to this and rolled their eyes because it only meant they would have to slay us harder. They ease up on you as time goes on in order to give the illusion of progress, and stop making you do pedantic things like tying and retying your boots over and over, but once they saw us enjoying ourselves a little too much, they came up with new games to play. Scuzz-brush the floor in duck-walk position for hours on end. Everybody touch the wall before the countdown (which always ran out). And then we were right back to crying and bickering, red-faced and swollen with misplaced rage.

Someone knocked the fire extinguisher off the wall by accident during one of the melee sessions and foam filled the air. In the midst of it all I began laughing uncontrollably at the sight of us pressed up against each other in squat position, straining to hold our scuzz brushes in the air as the DIs slowed their countdown to max out the pain.

What have we learned from boot camp? To kill? To be controlled? Have we been given a taste of simulated combat? Maybe. Or maybe we've just been formed into something separate from the rest of America, the disgusting things that will be herded eternally from one place to another, doing the stuff that makes other people shudder, and becoming ever more a part of something "bigger than ourselves."

When we graduate, a lot of the recruits are so proud they break down and cry as they're given their official Eagle, Globe, and Anchors.

Their blubbering faces make me sick.

Corporal Eamon comes over from his other platoon and congratulates us. His voice is totally different. The demon that once lived inside his larynx is gone and has been replaced with a normal-sounding man. This is extremely off-putting. He tells us he was only hard on us because we would have felt cheated if he wasn't. The validity of this statement rings truer than I expected.

Our senior DI, Gunnery Sergeant Soto, goes through and asks each of us what jobs we chose before we got there. Some are infantry, some are cooks, and quite a few joined with an open contract, which means they don't know what the fuck they're going to be doing for the next four years.

When he gets to me, he says, "Lagoze, you still look like your mom made you come here. What MOS are you?"

"Combat Camera, sir," I tell him.

"Why in the fuck would you choose that?" he asks.

"To keep the people informed, sir." I regret saying it the moment it comes out of my mouth.

"So you're gonna film Marines throwing puppies off of cliffs, huh?"

I have no idea what he's talking about.

"Yeah, I know your type. A blue falcon, a buddy fucker. You're gonna get other Marines in trouble."

"Aye, sir," I say.

⸻

As a treat, at the end of the show, we're allowed to watch a movie. We choose to watch *Jarhead*, a war film in which Marines watch other war films like *Apocalypse Now* and *Deer Hunter* in order to get themselves geared up for Desert Storm, a pseudo war that serves as a giant disappointment to them because it is nothing close to "the Nam." Matty and I fret over this. Could the same thing happen to us? Was it better to go to Iraq or Afghanistan? Will we miss the war by the time we get there? The clock is ticking.

Matty is infantry and I can see him drifting away from me because I am not infantry, and the ones who are have started banding together in the final few days. He'll see combat for sure, he tells me. It's in his job description. The word "Combat" is in mine, I tell him. He's not so sure.

"Maybe," he says. "If we do meet out there you gotta take a picture of me schwacking some motherfuckers."

"I got you," I assure him.

The DIs gather us around for one final campfire chat. They are our mentors now, and even smile occasionally as they look out at us, surveying the work they've done. Staff Sergeant Hert, our kill hat who has three Purple Hearts, regales us with a story about the time he killed a whole family in Iraq. They were at a checkpoint and a car came at them and wouldn't stop, even after warning shots were fired. Staff Sergeant Hert did what he had to do.

"That's the way it fuckin' goes, rah?"

"Oorah," we respond.

"Sometimes you're gonna kill women and kids."

"Why didn't they stop, Staff Sergeant?" someone asks nervously.

"I will never fuckin' know. Everything they do out there is ass backwards." He takes a pause to spit tobacco juice into a bottle sitting next to him. Everyone is quiet, as this is not the usual story they tell us. The usual stories are about women—good women, bad women, unfaithful women, treacherous women. Women who take all your money while you're on deployment and split.

"But," Staff Sergeant Hert continues, "one thing I'll never forget is the little girl in the backseat. Head was fuckin' split in half but she still had one eye open, just staring at me. Like a doll or something. That's the shit that haunts you, that you're gonna have to live with forever. You do what you gotta do to keep your fuckin' brothers alive."

In our minds it is clear that the family deserved it. They should've fucking stopped, or learned English before we invaded them. Now look at what they've done to Staff Sergeant Hert, one of the more reasonable kill hats we've had, who never made us do overly repetitive or heinous things like the others.

Gunnery Sergeant Soto breaks the silence:

"Just make sure Lagoze ain't filming when that shit happens to you, good to go?"

Everyone glares at me. It was a joke, I think, but no one's laughing. I'm a pariah, an outcast, a snitch who will only serve to get Marines court-martialed for doing what they had to do. And they know, deep down like Gunny Soto, that I haven't fully drunk the Kool-Aid during the past three months, that I am still Lagoze the Individual, the Yankee, the Jew from New York.

At the same time, however, I've never been a snitch. I assure myself that they've got me all wrong. Years later, after the war and the allegiances and friendships had faded, after we'd all been chewed up and spit out by the Marine Corps, and left to wallow in our memories and doubt, however, a snitch is exactly what I would become.

CHAPTER 3

The Schoolhouse

Fort Meade, Maryland, is cloistered by highways and woods, where signs for McDonald's come peeking out above the trees as you fly by on the nothing road of America. The woods in these parts of the country look as if you're seeing them from Google Maps Street View. They're washed out and monochromatic, and maybe that's the way the government wants to keep them. The National Security Agency (NSA) is on Fort Meade. Edward Snowden spent time there. It's also the home of the Defense Information School (DINFOS), where they send Combat Camera Marines to learn how to film war.

It's a lot like any other military installation; ugly, demoralizing, an abbreviated version of a town but instead of regular folks there are people dressed in digital camouflage everywhere. Occasionally you'll see a row of soldiers in a field with tripods and cameras, diddling with their new devices. To give you a sense of the level of security on the base, the Burger King was robbed twice while I was there.

"Remember that movie, 'I see dead people'?" He looked at us sideways from his computer chair. "Well, we don't just see them, we film them. That's the sexy part of our job. When you're not doing that, you're probably filming some bullshit ceremony or training op." Sergeant Ketcher, our combat videography instructor, stood up, then quickly sat back down. He seemed exasperated and slightly hungover. "I say this 'cause some of you probably didn't think you'd be getting shot at. 4671 Marine Videographer ... oh, that sounds fun. 'I'll take pictures of guys for promotion boards, or I'll make high-speed videos of the Navy conducting sea maneuvers, or maybe I'll get to fly around in a SuperCobra taking photos for aerial surveillance.' Nah, that ain't it."

He scratched his head crabbily.

"I mean, yeah, I guess sometimes we do that shit, but if you get put on a line company with the grunts you better be prepared to put up with the same shit as them."

Sergeant Ketcher bore the look of someone trying to appear jaded beyond his years, but I suspect he wouldn't have reenlisted and become a sergeant if he didn't secretly like the Marine Corps. He was skinny and fat at the same time, with a small pregnancy belly that poked out of the baggy, faded cammies he'd worn through multiple deployments. You start to see that being a Marine for a few years gives you the authority to treat those junior to you like morons. He hadn't been talking to us for more than five minutes but he was already weary.

"Standing post all night, filling sandbags, cleaning rifles. If you come up with some excuse not to carry your weight you just look like a POG."

A POG—person other than grunt—was the worst thing you could be called in the Marines. It was similar to desk jockey, which basically equated to being called a "pussy" by Marine standards. If you weren't infantry, you were doing something nonessential; it meant you weren't in the suck earning your paycheck. Suffering was a currency in the Marines—the more you suffered, the more respect you were given, the more complete you felt. Ironically, the infantry only made up around 10 percent of all military occupations, which meant there were a lot of men in uniform walking around with inferiority complexes.

Most importantly for us ComCam Marines, the infantry guys were the ones we had to woo so that we could get good footage of them. We were their fangirls, their roadies, the ones who would do anything to be accepted by them. They mystified us because they knew and saw things we didn't, and this elusiveness made them godlike in our eyes.

"It's not easy sometimes to get access," Ketcher went on. "Because, for some reason, there's a whole bunch of retards in Com-Cam who give the rest of us a bad rap. And all it takes is one."

"Yes, Sergeant," we agreed. It was the first day of class. You have to understand how tired everything feels after boot camp. Your brain still has a sleep debt from the past three months of waking up at 4 a.m. every morning, so by the time you get to the schoolhouse everything feels like a dream. On top of this, many of us hadn't finished growing yet, and our bodies were struggling to keep up. We were all pros at napping pretty much anywhere, catching a few extra z's whenever the opportunity presented itself.

"Wake up, bitch!" Ketcher flung a stress ball at Graves, whose head had kept dropping into his chest ("bobbing for cock," as our DIs called it). We all hissed at Graves, who looked around disoriented but indignantly at the rest of us. He used to be an emo kid and was still struggling to let that identity go. He disdained us, and we him.

"Despite there being an endless amount of fuckups and bullshit that we have to deal with, I'd still take our job over any other, any day of the week," he said. "Think about it. How many grunts have war stories? Every single one of 'em, right? Even the ones who've never been deployed." We chuckled. "But how many of them can *show you* their war stories? The rounds impacting next to them, the sound a JDAM makes as it goes flying through the air. 'Look, Mom, that's me crouched in a wadi waiting for the Taliban to drop a mortar.' " He let out a slow whistle that increased in volume, as if it would soon land on his desk. "That's what makes our job badass. We're bullshit-proof, no one can say shit to us. All I have to do . . ."

He clicked the mouse on his computer and pulled up a video on the large-screen projector at the head of the class.

"All I have to do is pull up a video I shot in Marjah," he said, hitting the play button.

A lone Marine kneels awkwardly on the roof of a mud hut holding an AT-4 rocket launcher. People shout incoherent things in the background, as Afghan moon dust floats around the lens of the camera, making the war look foreign, bleak, otherworldly. The war sounds and the screams reach a fever pitch until the rocket goes off, leaving behind a dull and anticlimactic thud that is overmodulated on the low-fi microphone Ketcher had been recording with. A lone voice in the background cheers half-heartedly.

It was a ten-second clip of basically nothing and was so shaky it looked like it was shot on a boat, but we were in awe, validated by our instructor's proof of his wartime experience, which in turn was proof that we weren't total POGs. For a generation that was just beginning to rely on video evidence to maintain our relevance in the world, to give sustenance to our dreams and our lived realities, these videos would be our path to the future, to the immortal yet disposable belief in documentation-as-existence. For Combat Camera kids, the camera was an extension of our rifles, a kill-shot-camcorder that doubled as both weapon and cataloger. Gotta catch 'em all, Pokémon.

———

Hämäläinen (pronounced "Ham-a-line-in") was either a Mormon or a Jehovah's Witness, I can't remember. He had joined the Marine Corps as a cameraman to showcase and preserve its fine, illustrious history. He was a real-life gee-willikers type, and it astounded me that these kids actually still existed, as if *Leave It to Beaver* had somehow been transposed into the new millennium through a combination of militant homeschooling and child locks.

He raised his hand with eyes eager and blue, chia pet hair shooting up from the high-and-tight haircut that accentuated his cuboid head. "Sergeant, I wanted to ask, I've heard that we'll be switching to digital cameras soon. I, uh . . . do you have any idea when that transition will take place or, um . . ?"

We all groaned at his perfectly valid question, and his response, a frantic series of shrugs, while going, "What? What? What?" just made it worse that he engaged with us.

"I don't know, Hämäläinen," Sergeant Ketcher said in a nasally whine. "But I'm sure the Army will get them before we do, like everything else."

"Aye, Sergeant," he said. "It's just . . . I feel like it would be, um, uh . . ?" (More groans.) "What? *What?* I just, I feel like it would be a good investment for Combat Camera to make, so we're not having to constantly change tapes in the field, and bring backups, and spend hours digitizing, and . . ." He made lots of unnecessary hand gestures and nervous chuckles to convey his point and justify his line of inquiry. Homeschooling was responsible for a lot of painfully awkward kids joining the Marines, and the fluster of Hämäläinen's sheltered upbringing was apparent in everything that he did: his movements, his speech and posture, even the way he did pull-ups. We ridiculed him mercilessly—because that's what we did—and eventually it would take its toll. I thought he was just nervous but actually he was very sad.

In the barracks on Fort Meade, they were always putting restrictions on us because we couldn't stop fucking each other. Students weren't allowed to have sex; we were supposed to wait until we got to our first duty stations. The female Marines were put on the second floor and we male Marines were on the third. Every night we'd sneak to each other's rooms, and each morning some kind of drama would play out and everyone would get punished as a result. If one woman had a beef with another, she would tell on her, or the higher-ups would find out from the person on duty, whose job it was to stay up all night patrolling the barracks looking for any late-night fuckery, then promptly log it into the "duty book." The guilty culprits would get marched out into the common area for a nonjudicial-punishment hearing, where our master sergeant would read off their crimes, then promptly berate us for not being able to keep it in our pants.

"Firth, how's it gonna look if you show up pregnant to your first duty station?"

"Not good, Mass Sergeant," she said, just days into her service as a Combat Lithographer and already near tears.

Back then, before everything was integrated and women were allowed into combat roles, that was the go-to excuse to bar them from certain places or doing certain things. Women couldn't deploy with the infantry because they would get pregnant, or they couldn't go on field ops because they'd get pregnant. You'd think birth control hadn't been invented yet in the Marines.

The guys who weren't getting laid were always fed up with the ones who were, tired of being punished for other people's sins. You could see the frustrations, sexual and otherwise, build up behind their eyes and inevitably harden into an intense, slut-shaming hatred. I was in a room with four of them and the stench was palpable.

"These fucking sluts can't wait till they get to the fleet?" Gibraltar asked furiously. He was always jerking off on the bunk above me, getting off to violent porn flicks where the women yelped in pain during their supposed first times doing anal. Sometimes he wouldn't even have the courtesy to cover himself with his poncho liner.

Morgan leered out from his corner of the room, which we had attempted to cordon off with shelves and desks to address his awful body odor problem, like stale death trapped inside a set of walking, talking cammies. Every morning after physical training and hygiene (Marine lingo for the showers), the squad leaders ran a body odor inspection on him, and if he still smelled they would force him back in for another round of cleaning. They even gave him a tutorial once on how to wash properly, acting like it was a huge burden on them, but clearly getting some kind of satisfaction out of forcing another man to strip down, shower, and hit a designated series of problem spots.

That was just one of the problems with Marines post–boot camp: we had grown addicted to watching each other get humiliated. Our TV was watching someone get chewed out for whatever infraction they had committed. We kept our ears fine-tuned to the frequency and pitch of a potential ass-chewing wherever we went, our sado-voyeuristic senses on high alert for the dulcet tones of a colleague getting ripped apart for not saluting an officer, or misrolling their sleeves.

"They haven't been getting any dick for the past five months, what do you expect?" Morgan said.

"Female Marines are nasty," Gibraltar spat. "I got an actual girl waiting for me in PA. I'm not risking getting a disease from these Wookiees."

It was safe here, because we didn't have to think too pressingly about the war yet. Most of us had accepted our fates when we signed the contract thinking we'd go straight to combat, and our death might happen quickly, like ripping a Band-Aid off. But the Marine Corps makes you wait, and in the waiting we forget our initial dive into the deep end. We wormed our way into complacency, like rats making a nest in a pile of shit.

———

Megan Duda got to Fort Meade the day after Private Howard hung himself in his room. He was the last kid you'd expect to do it, because he had seemed pretty happy-go-lucky during his time there. There were vague reasons for why he did it, but they didn't square up with his laid-back California vibe. It made you think there was something in the water.

"I heard his mom was sick," someone would say.

Whenever somebody killed themselves, we'd be forced to sit through a "suicide prevention class," where one of the instructors would come to the barracks and give us a PowerPoint presentation about not killing ourselves. This time Sergeant Ketcher came to do it, an odd choice given that he was one of the least uplifting people I'd ever met.

"Suicide is a permanent solution to a temporary problem," he droned, reading from the screen.

This was the first thing Duda saw when she got there: us huddled in the main common area next to the Ping-Pong table watching Ketcher struggle through his PowerPoint. We all gawked when she came in. It's hard to look good in camouflaged utilities—they're designed to hide curves and look as far from sexy as possible—but she really made it work.

Ketcher stared at her for a second, then went back to his presentation.

"Who knows what to say if you see another Marine looking depressed?" he asked.

"Ask them if they're okay, if they wanna talk, Sergeant?" someone guessed.

"Nah, just fuckin' ask them if they're gonna kill themselves. Don't beat around the bush."

It wasn't long before rumors started to swirl about our attention-grabbing new recruit. From here or there (most often, Gibraltar), fluid-soaked stories circulated of Duda in various rooms, positions, and configurations where sex and humiliation were one and the same. Out there women Marines became objects of scorn and confused fetishization; the equalizer and, to a camp full of confused boys wrestling with deep-set feelings of inadequacy, a thing to be dominated.

I saw her one cold morning out on the smoke pit and we talked for a bit. Her face was painted on pretty thick and her eyelash extensions made her eyes bug out like an anime character. She hugged her knees to her chest while smoking a Marlboro Red.

"It's fucking cold."

"Yeah," I said.

"Wish they'd let us wear our Gore-Tex."

"That would make too much sense."

She laughed and took a drag of her cigarette, shivering as she exhaled.

"Not as cold as it gets in Minnesota, though," she said, eyeing me to see if I would comment on her accent, which by now I thought she was putting on at least a little. I wondered if she knew about the rumors. I guessed she did, and that was one of the reasons she was playing up certain things. It's easier to embrace the roles that are handed out to us, the shut-in or slut or stoner, because to fight back against them is often a lose-lose situation. The Marines are no place for complicated origin stories.

"I know," she said. "My accent. Everybody's always making fun of me but I don't even notice it. It gets worse when I'm drunk." She took another drag. "You ever go to the bowling alley?" she asked.

We were all underage, so we had to sneak beers at the bowling alley on base.

"I've gone a couple times but it's kind of a shit show," I said.

"Well, yeah, 'cause you got people like Couture running around all the time," she scoffed. Couture was an Army chick whom we had all been briefed about the day we got to DINFOS. We were ordered to stay away from her because she was a walking STD, they said. At the moment, she was awaiting separation from the Army after a guy accused her of having sex with him without his consent in the bowling alley bathroom while he was passed out drunk. Couture would get to go home, but that was the wrong way. Would she figure something out about the world off base, back in reality? Would she be able to forget the things that happened to her while she was momentarily a soldier? Or would she become a meth addict?

I, on the other hand, was running eight miles a day, trying to work off the crushing regret and loneliness. "How did I end up here? And why must I die lonely when I'm only eighteen?" I would lament as I pushed deep into the woods that surrounded the base golf course, each turn and hill another tormenter to conquer. I was miserable. The problem with running away from things and creating new problems is that the old things never stay that way. They come back in waves of nostalgia.

I was working up the courage to ask Duda if she wanted to go to the bowling alley with me sometime, but before I could, Sergeant Ketcher came out to ruin the moment. Duda's eyes lit up when she saw him.

"Morning, Sergeant!" she called out to him.

"Jesus, Duda, why do you have to be so moto?" he said.

"I don't know, Sergeant. Just living the dream, I guess."

Ketcher groaned. I could tell Duda was into him and I felt stupid for assuming I'd had a chance with her. She was just another girl attracted to rank, I decided. As I was leaving, Ketcher called out to me.

"Hey, Lagoze, I wanna show you something later. Stay after class," he said.

"Okay, Sergeant," I said. Duda was watching Ketcher try to light his cigarette. She moved over to him and gave him cover from the wind, and I saw him flinch, then settle back and glance at her sideways.

When I got back to my room, Hämäläinen was there crying to Evans, another, slightly older Mormon or Jehovah's Witness who functioned as a role model for the other religious kids. He was trying to console Hämäläinen about God and the challenges that he presents us with.

"I just don't know what to do anymore," Hämäläinen was saying. "I called my dad and I didn't even have the courage to tell him what it's like here, what I've become. It would make him sick."

"Well, that's why you need God now more than ever," Evans said.

Hämäläinen stared off into the distance. "They keep making me do things. Last night they forced me to drink." Hämäläinen had made a scene the other night when the others got him drunk and

took him off the base into Baltimore. When they got back, someone had filmed as Hämäläinen lay on the floor outside one of the
female's rooms crying and professing his love for her.

"Did you tell them you can't drink?"

"Of course! Do you think they listen? 'God, you're such a faggot,
Hämäläinen. Don't be such a fucking pussy.' *See?*" he cried. "I've
even started cursing."

Hämäläinen let out a wail, then began to dry-heave. It would've
been sad if it wasn't so pathetic.

Evans put his hand on Hämäläinen's shoulder. "Why don't we
pray?" he asked.

Hämäläinen continued to cough and convulse as they bent
their heads.

Evans led: "Oh holy Father, please guide Hämäläinen during
this challenging time."

There was a knock at the door and I opened it. At first, I wasn't
sure what I was looking at. Two nude bodies stacked on top of each
other facing opposite directions in *Hop on Pop* fashion. When I
adjusted my eyes, I saw it was Taylor straddling Samson, a somber,
faceless Indiana boy who was bent over pantsless for maximum
exposure.

"What's wrong, Hämäläinen?" Taylor asked sweetly, using the
top of the doorway for support as he balanced on top of Samson.

Hämäläinen gave a look of utter defeat. "Hey, guys," he said,
wiping a tear away.

Taylor was a scumbag but Samson intrigued me. We'd been in
boot camp together and I'd hardly heard the guy say a word the
whole time until someone asked him why he was so quiet, to which
he replied, "I'm a sociopath."

He never smiled, never laughed, and I thought beneath the
stonelike exterior he was hiding some kind of brilliance. I wanted

to know his background but he wouldn't reveal anything. The most we talked about was our shared fondness for war literature, and I gave him my copy of Gustav Hasford's *The Short-Timers*, the basis for the movie *Full Metal Jacket*. He was obsessed with the main character, Private Joker, who was a Combat Correspondent in the Marines, like us. Since we'd gotten to DINFOS, however, he'd been hijacked by some of the more senior guys, who saw the strange mask he wore as an opportunity to parade him around like some kind of psychotic mascot. We'd go running past the Army and Air Force barracks at five in the morning, and they'd have him do insane chants to wake them all up. Sometimes he would just stand outside their rooms screaming, in a style I struggled to believe was being done in anything but absolute sincerity. I thought there had to be a history there, for sure, but no one cared to really look.

———

Ketcher and Duda were found out right before we were set to graduate from our video production class. Sleeping with students was a big no-no; it was already fraternization for people who outranked each other to date or even hang out, so Ketcher was busted down and lost his teaching position. Duda was only a private and couldn't be busted down any further, so our master sergeant cut her pay and put her on restriction; she wasn't allowed to leave her room except to go to class and the chow hall. She was prescribed antidepressants and sleeping pills from the base therapist, and her roommates were supposed to keep an eye on her, but someone kept sneaking her booze. She got caught in another guy's room a couple of weeks later and they started filing the paperwork to have her separated from the Marine Corps.

"You will not be able to tell people you were a Marine, Duda," our master sergeant told her at her hearing. "You never completed your training, you never made it to the fleet." She looked like she didn't even know where she was. She had gained a lot of weight in the past few weeks and her face was all puffy from lack of sleep.

"I'd still fuck her," Morgan said after the hearing. I wanted to deck him in the face but I was worried his stink might get on me.

Ketcher had never showed me whatever he'd wanted to show me. I saw him one morning at the chow hall and went to sit with him for old times' sake before he left the base. He sat up straight and told me to come by his room later; he couldn't be seen hanging around the students. His stuff was all packed up when I got there, except for an Xbox that was plugged into a small TV. The teachers lived in a slightly nicer barracks but it was still pretty depressing. For his part, Ketcher seemed excited to be leaving Fort Meade and going back to the fleet, then eventually Afghanistan. We didn't mention Duda, which was kind of the point, I guess.

"I can't show you guys this stuff in class because it's too fucked-up crazy," he said, pulling out a hard drive. "You'd have someone like Hämäläinen crying to Mass Sergeant."

He plugged in the hard drive to his laptop and opened a file called "Porn."

"But I can tell you're not here to film change-of-command ceremonies. You wanna get to the war," he said. "You look like a killer, Lagoze. The grunts will respect you as long as you keep your attitude in check."

"Aye, Sergeant," I said. I wondered what it meant to look like a killer. Or if he knew that my attitude was not merely a problem with authority but a resentment for everything the Marine Corps stood for, and that my being in uniform was still largely a mystery, even to myself. He was right about one thing, though: I needed to get to the war. It was the only thing keeping me going, the idea of hitting the reset button, getting washed clean by the experience.

That's how much I had riding on it. In that sense, I thought Samson, the sociopath, and I were similar; we were both just going through the motions in order to make it to higher ground. The military was a portal for us, a means to an end. Fuck everything else.

The videos he wanted to show me were from Iraq. They were filmed by a previous instructor at DINFOS, Staff Sergeant Kenyon, who had given them to Ketcher as a kind of calling card—proof that he was the shit. It was some of the heaviest stuff I'd ever seen captured on camera:

> A group of Marines stand against a wall. As they throw frags over it and into a courtyard area, the screams of an enemy fighter can be heard between the constant hammering of the grenades. Next, a cut to the aftermath: a dead fighter splayed in the courtyard, blood soaked and ripped apart. It was a dogfight, and the Marines in the video look buoyant in their raggedness as they moved through the dusty, gray streets of Anywhere, War. Americans do it best.
>
> One guy does a 360 spin on his heel before they enter a building with guns at the ready. Inside is what appears to be an Iraqi Army torture house, where a charred body sits chained to a chair, looking like a fucked-up exhibit from the Museum of Modern Art.

The videos of beheadings they trained us on in boot camp and the "Allahu akbars" that propagated news channels back home created a myth of the insurgent as a ghoul-like creature, larger than life but parasitic in intent. They condensed the whole thing into a battle of good and evil, which might have been the evilest thing of all. But this was the first time I'd actually heard the enemy's voices cry out in pain in the heat of battle, and I was unsettled by how banal it sounded. *This* was the stuff they made us do chants about? "Operation Phantom Fury—house to house, street to street." Ketcher looked on at me, waiting for my reaction:

> Marines mill around a body, their faces not adequately registering what they are looking at. They seem almost bored. The guy who did a spin smiles in the background at something happening off camera. Then evidence-oriented shots: the body, the tools used.
>
> Now, a firefight. There doesn't seem to be any order to the events. Guns and commands shouted inside a cramped room, thrown off by a random question someone would ask between magazine changes. "Where's fucking Gallagher?"
>
> Things quiet down before a quick shot of a dead Marine being dragged just out of view behind a door, leaving behind a thick red trail—shot secretly, as if the camera is only now revealing too much.
>
> It ends the same way it began, nihilistically, with a Marine ramming his buttstock into a mirror in an Iraqi bedroom, shattering the glass. This, edited in slow motion, a hackneyed attempt to impart poetic meaning

as if it were something other than another angsty
White kid at war living out his tortured fantasy. There
is a quick shot to close it out in night vision: a sleeping
Marine being tea-bagged, so fast you'd miss it if you
blinked (Staff Sergeant Kenyon's own little auteur touch),
and then the montage goes to black.

It felt like I'd gained access to something forbidden by American hegemony, like the underground labs of Area 51, something mystical and accessible only to those who were immortal in their connections and power. It was incredible that this stuff was just sitting on Ketcher's laptop, a mere E-6 in the lower echelons of the military-industrial complex. We too could be omniscient. Like everything in the military, the videos dared us not to care. You think you're hard? Try watching videos of real death and acting turned on by them. It's not enough to be tough; the American male psyche is, at its root, haunted by sadism.

"Are you going to do anything with this stuff?" I asked him.

"Like what?"

"I don't know. Maybe you could give it to a museum or film archive or something. It seems historical."

"Are you kidding?" he said. "People would lose their shit if they saw this. They'd call us monsters, or worse, they'd think we were damaged beyond repair. I can't even tell civilians half the shit I've seen 'cause they look at me like I'm fucking crazy. You think you could get a job in the real world after showing someone this?"

I guess he had a point, but, like everything with Ketcher, he seemed to be holding his cards a little close to the chest, as if they might go floating away if he revealed them in the slightest.

He would never do anything with the footage. I know because I still search for it occasionally, scouring the war porn sites of the dirty web, stumbling upon other equally shocking videos. It had somehow escaped the tendrils of the internet to live only in the memories of the few people who had witnessed it, which was kind of comforting, that that could still happen.

———

Duda overdosed on the pills she'd been prescribed the week we were set to leave. I remember the morning that the ambulance came to the barracks and the concerned looks on her roommates' faces. She survived, luckily, and they started expediting the process of her discharge. She didn't have to hear other people's shit for the rest of the time she was there, and she walked around the barracks freely in her pajamas, giving everyone the cold shoulder. I thought, *good for her*, but all the other females cursed her behind her back. She was giving the rest of them a bad rap. I learned from some of them that their version of boot camp involved a lot of the women drill instructors telling them that they would never amount to anything other than what we, the men on base, expected them to be. Sex objects, free for the taking. Gibraltar couldn't have been more pleased.

After graduating I got sent to Okinawa, Japan, to wait some more. Samson got stationed at Quantico, Virginia, where I heard he jumped in front of a train shortly after he arrived. I still have the copy of *The Short-Timers* I had given him. In it he had underlined a passage where Private Joker arrives at Parris Island and they're waiting to meet their drill instructors. He turns to another recruit and says, "I don't think I'm going to like this movie."

I wasn't sad, really, just more intrigued by the *enigma* of Samson. When you're eighteen, suicide feels like the ballsiest thing you can do. It showed that the history behind Samson I'd suspected existed was tried and true. He was missing something inside him, and that triggered the arsonist in me, the kid afraid to love because I never felt that I deserved to be loved myself.

It didn't matter. In a year I would be someone new anyway.

CHAPTER 4

Sad Bois in Paradise

They tell you lots of things before you go places. They tell you about the prostitutes in Thailand, the banana show in Oki. They tell you about the best strip clubs in Pendleton, and the worst ones in Jacksonville, North Carolina. "Toby's for sure. I saw a bitch literally about to give birth onstage once, I shit you not." They tell you how it is to deploy, your seniors, instructors, friends; Iraq and Afghanistan meld into the same place. They talk about the camel spiders and scorpions, how it gets so hot you can drink eight bottles of water and still not have to pee because it'll sweat right through you and your gear. They tell you how dead bodies look after civilian equipment, like a compact sedan, gets torn apart by gunfire with a family inside. They tell you about the hash, primo stuff, and how you're still a boot (a nobody, an amateur) till you get high in the middle of a firefight. They tell you vague and contradictory things that make you feel less prepared than you did before, and they build it all up until you start to wonder if it's real or if the same stories aren't just getting passed from Marine to Marine.

What is combat? Is it driving and getting blown up? Is it walking and getting shot? Is it getting mortared inside a porta-potty? Trying to understand what a firefight felt like before going was like asking a virgin to explain what sex felt like. It *was* sexual, of course, but it was also paralysis inducing. "You 'member when fuckin' Chambers froze up in the middle of that road? Had to tackle him into a wadi. We had a field day with him after that." They beat the shit out of you if you froze up; freezing up was worse than death. And if you were a POG? Oh boy, you'd better hope it didn't happen to you while you were with a line company.

They make you do chants to distance yourself from your former civilian self, like, *I went to the mall, where all the fatties shop, I pulled out my machete, and I began to chop. I went to the playground, where all the kiddies play, I pulled out my machine gun, and I began to spray.* And they reiterate to you how terrible women are, how guys come back from deployments to wives impregnated by other guys, or who had become strippers out in town, or just emptied their husbands' bank accounts and split. Women Marines, those who had the audacity to think they could be Marines, got it even worse.

But you're not a Marine until you do what Marines do, which is go to war. Earn your stripes, get your Combat Action Ribbon. The mental distance necessary to pack away the worst of the worst. I'd seen more trauma registered in guys who had spent their four years waiting to deploy and never going than those who did multiple tours. Ashamed to even tell people they had served, they would get discharged and look back at those years as a giant wash and think, *What did I put myself through?*

I had been in Okinawa for a year before they sent me to Camp Lejeune, North Carolina. I had to complain to the higher-ups every day until they slated me to deploy to combat. Everything was totally arbitrary in the Marines; it wasn't the few or the proud who they sent to the war, just whoever happened to be in the right place at the right time.

People in the States say they support the troops, but anyone who's actually lived near us and had to deal with us knows that we're all assholes. We were a fraternity of killers, but in Japan, where there wasn't anyone to kill, we put all of our energies into convincing the local women to sleep with us. We'd take a *honcho*, slang for taxi, into Naha, the capital of Okinawa, and walk around doing the imperialist ditty-bop. I could be anyone or anything a girl wanted me to be: cute, funny, complicated, a total simpleton. We would communicate with them via their phones, which had a translation app that would often make things more confusing, and then we'd go to a love hotel and have sex in the dark and when I'd wake up the next morning, they'd be looking at me like, "What are you still doing here?"

"Yellow fever" was the driving force in our empty lives, the reason we still occupied Japan, so that Marines could enjoy the fruits of a culture and people traumatized by World War II, and by our subsequent occupations and wars in which they served as an R&R port for troops returning from combat in Korea and Vietnam. A lot of the old bartenders in Okinawa had stories about when the island was divided by race, and Black Marines had a separate red-light district from Whites.

I met Isabella, a woman from Fukuoka, after a period where I'd been going out at night by myself almost every day after work, staying out till 5 a.m., when the Marine guards were replaced by the Japanese ones, then sneaking back onto the base so as to avoid punishment. Enlisted Marines weren't allowed to stay off base past midnight, rules imposed after three-too-many "international incidents" over the years: the time a group of Marines raped and killed a twelve-year-old girl in Okinawa, the time a sailor supposedly stole a tank and crashed it into the seawall, the time a Marine got blackout drunk and broke into someone's house and was found naked in the family's fifteen-year-old daughter's bedroom. I respected that the rules had been earned and justified, but the culturelessness of Camp Foster (where the only thing to do was go bowling, get drunk at the E-Club, or rent movies from the library) did not help to keep this age demographic of soldiers under control, while there was an entire country literally bursting with life just outside the fence. From my window in the barracks, I could see the beach and the Ferris wheel in Chatan's American Village. There seemed to be, to me at least, a secret brimming under the surface of the island, a crazy kind of slum hidden beneath a paradisiacal resort place for Japanese tourists and wannabe colonists from across the sea. There were dark histories and undertones, a story in every pachinko and lurking behind every alleyway. Children inexplicably roamed the streets at all hours without any parental figures in sight. The island was trying to give off brochure vibes but I was getting more *Enter the Void* or Takeshi Kitano currents.

The night started with me crashing a karaoke party in a snack bar that the locals begrudgingly allowed me entrance to, then getting stalked through the streets by an elderly man who kept shouting, "Hey, GI! Fuck! GI! Fuck!" until I was pushed into a cab around eight in the morning by a young Rastafarian type who had sold me fake weed. Isabella, already inside, looked at me and, without any introduction, said the magic words.

"I want to go to Taco Bell."

She was at least ten years older than me. You could barely tell except for under the eyes; she had eye shadow painted on so thick that it formed little mounds under them, like black tea bags. Huge eyes that stared at you from some forgotten place.

The only Taco Bell on the island was on Camp Foster—which I happened to live on, I told her—but first I would need to get some sleep. I would have to escort her because the locals weren't allowed on the base unaccompanied by a Marine. She nodded solemnly. I don't remember what we talked about, or if we talked about anything during the cab ride, but I do remember seeing her smile and hearing her strange Pillsbury Doughboy laugh for the first time as we got closer to the base. It was the laugh that made me want to die.

We got to the barracks and I snuck her into my room through a side stairwell and then passed out, feeling physically sick as I was, and when I woke up, I found her sitting on the bed next to me with a burrito in hand, scrunching her face distastefully.

I jumped out of bed. "How'd you get that?" I asked.

She just looked at me and widened her already wide eyes. "Hm?" she said.

"How did you get that burrito?"

"I went to Taco Bell."

"Nobody stopped you?"

She just shook her head. She seemed confused by my alarm, but I tried to explain that I could have gotten in serious trouble if it was found out that she'd been in my room, or that she'd walked unaccompanied to Taco Bell. Women, even women Marines, weren't allowed in our rooms with a closed door if they wanted to hang out. Not to say it was well enforced, but there was a no-sex-in-the-barracks policy.

"Well, what do you think?" I asked, nodding at the burrito.

"Not . . . good," she said.

I laughed. "No shit. You should have gotten the breakfast burrito. They put little potato bits in it; it's actually not that bad."

She pointed to the other side of the room at the human skull my roommate, Tim Dirkson, had found in the jungle one night.

Dirkson was basically a feral person. He was actually *too much* of an outdoorsman for the Marine Corps. Dirkson was always complaining about the rudimentary survival skills training we received. Even Jungle Warfare Training at Camp Gonzalez, where he'd photographed Marines rapelling down slimy rock walls and swimming through muddy streams for recruitment posters, was "fucking gay" in his eyes.

"They brought in a goat and slit its throat. Didn't even hunt it or anything," he said after he'd gotten back from the monthlong exercise.

"What the fuck is a goat doing in the jungle?" I replied.

He found his own way of testing himself and would sneak off base past midnight, like me, but instead of going clubbing, he would take a bus up north as far as it would go, then escape into the jungle with just a sleeping bag and a bottle of Suntory to spend the night among the habu snakes.

Apparently, he'd been showing Isabella the skull while I was passed out, but she couldn't understand anything through his low and crackly growls. He sounded exactly, and I mean spot-on, like the voice of Krumm from that Nickelodeon show *Aaahh!!! Real Monsters*.

Isabella picked up the skull and examined it.

"Yeah, I've been trying to get him to take that back wherever he found it," I said.

"I think it's from a shrine," she said.

"Oh, shit," I said. There were a lot of things left over from the Battle of Okinawa that we were warned to stay away from, like old land mines and suicide caves where people had gone to kill themselves before the Americans invaded. "He needs to put that back where he found it," I said. She just shrugged and put it back on top of Dirkson's iMac, used mainly for drawing graphic designs of said skull.

Born Ichika (Isabella was a pseudonym I never did quite figure out), she spoke English well enough because she had run away to France when she was sixteen, then London, and had generally steered clear of Japan and her family for many years. She found Japanese culture repressive, and whenever we were turned away from some activity by a ticket salesman (the time we tried to board a ferry to Ie Island to go whale watching, but were told the weather was too rough), or car rental clerk (the time we tried to rent a scooter, but Isabella didn't have the right license), she would turn to me, shake her head, and say, "Fucking Japs, man."

She was so obviously my manic pixie dream girl, and there was something bad that had happened to her that I was too dumb and selfish to fully realize during our time together. She was a bit too manic. Sometimes we'd be walking down the street and she'd abruptly veer into oncoming traffic, as if in direct revolt against even the most fundamental laws that Japanese society imposed. I would have to run into the street and yank her back, after which I'd stare at her bewilderedly.

"Why do you keep doing that?" I'd ask.

"It's okay" was all she'd say.

———

Ichika had some strange pills she'd been prescribed from a doctor that made her even loopier, and tired. She would sleep for days in my barracks room, and I would come back from work at the base Combat Camera shop (where we'd while away time filming vacuous bullshit like change-of-command ceremonies) to find her waiting for me with a mystery smile, applying eye shadow onto the bags under her eyes that never seemed to go away, no matter how much sleep she got.

In hindsight she was probably hurting from the man she'd left behind in the United Kingdom. As a couple, they had endured multiple miscarriages, and the guy's domineering mother, whom they lived with, didn't approve of Isabella. From what limited information I could get out of her, she'd gone to Okinawa to clear her mind. Sometimes when we'd pass by some kids she would stop and play with them, then later start crying. I was nineteen, though, and plenty capable of cheering her up and providing as many youthful distractions from her past life as she could hope for. We went everywhere together and she was game for pretty much anything, even when Dirkson wanted to go jumping off bridges in Nago, or steal whiskey and dried octopus from a Lawson convenience store (she would distract the clerks by asking them circular questions). Although I loved her—maybe wasn't in love with her, but had strong feelings, nonetheless—I couldn't shake the feeling that she thought I was just using her as some kind of tour guide/badge of honor. Which I basically was. Sixty percent of my reason for dating women in Japan was to show them off to my friends as well as other locals, proving that I wasn't just your average *gaijin*—while not having the self-awareness to see that I was making myself even more of a *gaijin* by doing so.

When Dirkson got sent to Camp Pendleton in California and I got Garcia as my new roommate, I was excited because he was even more into going out and partying than I was. Garcia had just come off the Marine Expeditionary Unit, where he'd been floating on a ship for several months in the Pacific, docking in various places like the Philippines and Thailand, and tearing through as many prostitutes as he could find. He was probably the most performatively masculine guy you could find in Combat Camera, evidenced by the fact that, although having been a videographer for two years by the time I met him, he still didn't know how to use a camera. He occupied himself on ship by doing things with the recon guys, or getting into fights with people he perceived as disrespecting him. Once, after they had briefly docked in Singapore to refuel, Garcia had run off the ship to grab a pizza at a Papa Johns. Back on board, he'd left it sitting on his rack for a few minutes and came back to find it half-eaten. He went thrashing through people's lockers while frothing at the mouth, swearing to kill whoever had eaten it until he had to be temporarily restrained and given a psychiatric evaluation before the ship could take off again.

But ship life did weird things to Marines sometimes. To me, he felt like something of an old-school Marlon Brando type. A bull loose in a pen; the kind of guy you couldn't argue with; you just had to shut up and go along with whatever Garcia wanted that day. He said most of his problems stemmed from growing up without his father around, an abusive womanizer he still idolized after he had left him when he was a kid with his mom in Las Vegas. He was always hinting—never outright saying, of course—that his old man had been some kind of contract killer for the mafia back in the day, but I didn't buy it.

We would sell Spice, the artificial marijuana substitute, and Bron, a Japanese brand of cough medicine that contained actual codeine, out of our room, and we started an underground distribution system for fake gold cards—after-hours passes—for lance corporals who wouldn't otherwise be able to stay off base. (Gold cards were for noncommissioned officers, or NCOs, and officers who could stay out past midnight—you had to show them to the guards when you came back on base—while red cards were for us lowly E-3s and below.) Garcia made a habit of walking around our room with his gut hanging out of a wifebeater, spraying air freshener obsessively and blasting Alicia Keys's "Try Sleeping with a Broken Heart" while we all smoked and talked about much we hated the Marine Corps. One time he got so Spiced and Bron'd out that he claimed he saw the devil, and lay paralyzed with his face frozen in terror in his rack, the rest of us laughing hysterically at him, until we saw a single tear come rolling off his eye.

Garcia had been having panic attacks about this Navy girl he was seeing, a hospital corpsman who'd been cool enough to reset my nose after I'd blacked out one night and gotten it busted by some supply Marines who were acting stupid (you couldn't go to medical for fight injuries because they would charge you with "destruction of government property," so she did it for me in the barracks). She had recently informed Garcia that she was pregnant, and he was having a very difficult time accepting this, thinking about his father and his own childhood. He would go through bouts of extreme anxiety and depression, where he would insist we go to Soap Land, the red-light district, so that he could forget about his worries, if only for a few hours.

It wasn't long before he was insisting that I share Isabella with him, as if it wasn't even up to her, but solely my discretion.

"No, dude," I said. "She's my girlfriend, not a prostitute."

"Japanese girls don't count as girlfriends," he said bluntly with a condescending smile, as if I still had so much to learn. At this point, Isabella was practically living in our room, which was the size of a single bedroom with shelves and desks used to separate our two sides. She was spending most of her time lounging around in her underwear, after I'd finally instilled it into her that she couldn't leave the room without me. We had stopped going out as much, because I was awaiting orders to Camp Lejeune, North Carolina, wherefrom, they told me, I would be going straight to Afghanistan. So I was mentally preparing for that, getting in reps of *Call of Duty* in this other guy's room, and too often leaving her in my and Garcia's room bored out of her fucking mind.

One day while I was at work, I got a text from her that said

help. I quickly rushed back to the barracks, expecting the sergeant on duty to be there questioning what she was doing in our room. Instead I found Brady, another guy from the shop, sitting on my bed with her.

"What are you doing?" I asked him.

"Oh, shit, what's up, man," he said, giving me a hug and dapping me up. "Garcia said I should come by, dude. Don't stress. I'm on my way out." He grabbed his phone and left chuckling.

I asked Isabella what happened, what he'd been doing there, and she sighed and put her hand under my shirt and started rubbing my chest, while giving me a kind of exasperated look. She told me she couldn't cry for help because she didn't want me to get in trouble. I was livid, but also sort of helpless. When Garcia got off work, I said he couldn't be giving our room key to random dudes, inviting them to try to rape my girlfriend.

Then, like a background character in a video game awaiting a triggered action, a switch flipped in his head, and he went ballistic. "SHE CAN'T BE IN HERE WALKING AROUND IN HER FUCKIN' UNDERWEAR, AND NOT EXPECT SHIT LIKE THIS TO HAPPEN."

"What?" was all I could say, before he knocked me to the ground.

"Get the fuck outta my face, bitch," he said, going past me into the hallway. I went after him, but again, he pushed me down. Garcia was a big guy, and he had the upper hand because of how shocked and betrayed I felt. I honestly thought he was my friend, and I couldn't muster up enough anger out of the hurt to do any real harm.

When he moved out a few days later, he just shook his head sadly at me. "I can't live with you, bro. When I saw you lying on the floor like that after I barely pushed you, I just felt bad for you. I can't be around someone I pity like that."

My next roommate was Janus, a shy little hermit of a kid with such severe acne he had to sleep on his back without his face touching the pillow, and who wrote his daily schedule down on a piece of paper (wake up, brush teeth, eat breakfast—tedious shit like that) and put it on our fridge each morning, and who spoke out of a small hole in the side of his mouth. I obviously felt more secure keeping Isabella there, but a fucked-up part of me missed Garcia.

As my PCS date (move date) to Lejeune grew closer, Isabella and I started going out even less. There were half-baked suggestions of us getting married so she could come with me, but when I thought of her in North Carolina, my heart sank. I pictured her withering away in some empty, shithole town outside of Jacksonville getting more unwell than she already was. Isabella's magic would not be able to sustain itself in a place like that.

Our last night together, I yelled at her because she left my room again without me. She wanted to go say good-bye to our now-mutual friends. She was crying fat globs of tears that were shattering the little mountains under her eyes when I put her in a *honcho*, and I hated her because I hated myself.

Years later, a friend of mine told me he'd once found Garcia and Brady and another guy in our room assaulting her while I was at work—a sad, resigned look in her eyes while they did it—and he'd had to physically remove her to his room and lock the door so she would be safe. All I could do was think about what a piece of shit I'd been not to do anything about it.

Isabella disappeared after that last night we were together. I couldn't find her on social media, and I wondered if even her Japanese name had been a fake. I thought about her specter of a personality drifting through the world unseen, unreachable, and I worried. It wouldn't be for another eight years or so that I'd track her down on Flickr, and there she was, happily married with three kids. She'd gotten back together with that British guy. I almost didn't recognize her at first; the black tea bags under her eyes were gone and she looked much healthier and more youthful than when I had known her. I thought about reaching out but decided not to. I could only do more harm.

———

When I finally got orders to go to Afghanistan, I felt less ready than I did when I was in high school. The radical, borderline religious fringe elements of my ideology had diminished significantly, and I was more concerned about the logistics of the thing, where we would be and for how long, what the living accommodations would look like.

Lance Corporal Loya, my team leader and fellow photographer, did his best to make sense of it to me. "It's like a really long, messed-up camping trip," he said. "At first it seems like it's never going to end, but then, before you know it, it's over."

I liked Loya, as everyone did. You knew because anytime someone met him, they'd tell you, "I like that guy." He was spiritual, in the sense that in high school he would drop acid and take ecstasy in the deserts of El Paso, and would feel the presence of God with such assuredness that he could convince you, too. He had a purity that instilled faith in the human race, and when I found myself thinking everyone was full of shit (especially after my dealings with Garcia), I just had to remember that there were people like Loya who would actually die for you. On top of that, he never jerked off; he thought porn was wrong. In an organization that literally survived on porn (there were guys with whole terabytes of the wildest stuff you could imagine), that had to mean something.

Before the operation started, Loya and I stood in an air-conditioned room on Camp Leatherneck, a giant Forward Operating Base that once existed in the middle of the desert in Afghanistan's Helmand Province, listening to our commanding officer, Chief Warrant Officer Walsh, wax lyrical about the infinite joys of being Combat Camera.

"We get to do it all," he said, beaming with satisfaction. "If Air needs us, we go with Air. Artillery, so be it. Hell, we even got Com-Cam attaching to MARSOC—Marine Forces Special Operations Command—right now." But, he told us, Loya and I were especially lucky because we were getting attached to an infantry unit for one of the last clearing operations conducted by U.S. forces in the region. "Tell me you guys are stoked. Are you stoked or what?" He sat there grinning, hair gelled back like a lot of officers do, a salesman selling motivation. On his desk was a drawing someone had made for him of an eagle dressed in cammies touting both a rifle and a camera, the unofficial mascot of our occupational specialty. Next to it was a photo of himself on patrol, walking knee-deep through a wadi with his camera in hand, a documenter being documented. It was probably the only patrol he'd ever been on, so he wanted to make sure someone got a shot of him.

The purpose of Combat Camera, once you were on the ground and actually filming stuff, was not entirely clear. If we needed to get an interview with someone, their first question would usually be, "Where's this video gonna go?"

I often wouldn't have the answer. Most of it got archived, shuffled into a database so some colonel working at a desk in Quantico could get a glimpse of what the war was looking like on the ground. If it was deemed suitable for public release, then it would get uploaded by Walsh onto the Defense Visual Information Distribution Service (DVIDShub.net), where you can find an endless stream of Christmas and Thanksgiving shout-outs from soldiers and sailors wishing their families back home a Merry Christmas and happy holidays from Afghanistan—Tennessee drawls telling their wives to "give lil' Destiny a hug for me, I'll be home soon."

If you were lucky, your video would get broadcast on AFN, the American Forces Network, a news station created by and for the military—a strange feedback loop of cheerful nonsense, too hokey to even be considered propaganda—that was persistently beamed out to the troops. Mostly it was seen as a joke or completely ignored, played in the background at mess halls on air bases in Bagram, or Italy, or Kurdistan. "Today, airmen with the Eighteenth Wing stationed on Kadena Air Base in Okinawa, Japan, got a special treat," I once had to narrate. "A volleyball match between Japanese police officers and Air Force MPs. What started out as a serious competition soon turned to laughs, as Okinawan locals joined in on the fun...." You wouldn't even know America was at war if you were tuned in to AFN.

Walsh kept grinning, looking at us as if he was expecting some kind of assurance that we weren't going to fuck this up, that we would not tarnish the sacred and wholesome name of what he referred to as the "Combat Camera Family."

"We're pretty stoked, sir," Loya and I said.

He nodded sagely. "Now, I'm sure you guys want to get out there into the fight and get some badass imagery of Marines hooking and jabbing, but it's not always about kicking in doors and sending rounds downrange, right? We're starting to transition *out of* Afghanistan right now, and our imagery needs to reflect that. So, what does that mean for ComCam?" he asked, waiting like a schoolteacher for us to give him the correct answer.

We both stood at parade rest. I looked over at Loya, who, although we were the same rank, was my senior because he had already deployed once before. He cleared his throat.

"Um," he said. "Just . . . you know, hearts and minds, sir. Hearts and minds . . ." He trailed off, losing focus. We were both feeling pretty shaky that morning, having drunk an entire case of Robitussin cough syrup the night before.

Walsh raised his eyebrows dubiously. "Hearts and minds, yeah. But even more important is our joint cooperation with the Afghan Army. We need people to see that the ANA is a dependable fighting force, capable of taking on the Taliban once we leave. That means shots of them patrolling, working together with Marines, even taking the lead. Most of your captions are going to read, 'Afghan led' on this one. . . ." He went on for a while longer.

It had been a stupid idea, as Robotripping always was, but it was Matty's idea, so we went along with it. Matty Burgos was a machine gunner with the Scout Sniper platoon whom I knew from boot camp. He was half Puerto Rican and half White, born and raised in Perth Amboy, a dirty New Jersey suburb where his dad had been a heroin addict who'd gotten himself tossed out of a projects window when Matty was a kid. Much like Garcia, he was both impossible to deal with and impossible to keep away from at the same time. We called him "the Politician" because he had two faces: one he presented to higher-ups and other general straights in the Corps, which was a real Marine's Marine type of bro persona, and the other one that came out in the giddy night, which was like Doctor Gonzo on some new kind of drug he had yet to experiment with.

"Why," we had asked him, "why would we possibly want to get high off some cheap-ass, low-grade-type pharmacy shit like Robitussin cough syrup? And out here in the desert?"

Matty just smiled wide with dimples creasing to the outer edges of his face, turning his eyes into crablike slits, a Puerto Rican Heath Ledger. "We're wilding 'cause we're *young, bro*," he said.

It was imperative for us to get wasted one last time before the deployment started, since we had all sort of acknowledged—not explicitly, just physically, in a dark corner of our lower intestines—that we were going to die. In that way, and that way only, the young and invincible face their own mortality; in small, subtle waves of physical dread that get quietly pushed aside, swallowed down after a slight cognitive reset that puts the heartbeat back on its normal pace. *It's not gonna be me*, you think. *But that would suck if it was.*

Forward Operating Bases, or FOBs, were the luxury resorts of deployments, a staging ground for combat troops about to head out to wherever the fight was, and a permanent residence for thousands of noncombat personnel and civilian contractors. Camp Leatherneck, also known as Camp Cupcake, was the Hilton of FOBs. It had a Pizza Hut, a KFC, and a Starbucks. It was the embodiment of a country that had been at war for so long that it had gotten overly comfortable. It was the only place that had a PX where you could indulge in all the amenities of home, and, as Matty also pointed out, it was the last time we'd see any women for the next seven months.

"After this, it'll be nothing but hajis," he said. "And I don't think we're allowed to fuck with the hajis."

"Definitely against standard operating procedures," Loya said.

Robitussin was the only option for us, as alcohol was contraband for service members, and it was the only drug they sold on base that could actually get you fucked up. After each of us purchased our share, getting strange looks from the civilian contractors who ran the PX, we went off into an empty dirt field. Under the stadium lights that illuminated the place, we downed the nasty medicine with slugs of Sprite to chase it, Matty constantly on the lookout for any approaching Marines. Loya threw up almost immediately. We both chastised him, telling him it would diminish his high, and he downed some more.

Eventually we began to hobble through the desert, heading where, we weren't exactly sure, but as the drug began to set in, we knew we had to steer clear of other Marines. We could not be seen in this state: shriveled and shrunken, our eyes cast downward so as not to face the glaring lights around us, giggling occasionally at the absurdity of what we were—Marines in a war zone. Soon enough, however, we ended up surrounded by people. Matty had mentioned some kind of dance going on at the Morale, Welfare, and Recreation center, located near the permanent residence huts that the Fobbits—the Marines who lived on the FOB—occupied.

When we walked up to the place, an old air hangar that had been converted into a rec center, I could hear Toby Keith coming from the loudspeaker inside and I knew that this was a bad place to be. Matty pushed open the door, and I was blinded momentarily by the fluorescent lights. When I reopened my eyes, I saw staff sergeants and gunnies, air wingers and other Fobbits lining the walls with arms crossed, watching a square-dancing competition that was taking place in the center of the floor.

There were only four or five women dancing, and well over thirty dudes trying to get in on the action. In the ring, the few country boys who actually knew how to dance were swinging their partners around with a fervor that could only come from having been trapped in the desert for too long, competing hopelessly over the same handful of women who lived on the base. It was an awful sight to witness, and I began to feel sick.

We had gotten about ten steps into the place when a gunnery sergeant spotted Matty. "Ey, Marine," he said as we went walking by. Matty was grinning like a nutcase. I decided I'd skip out on the colossal ass-chewing that was about to unfold and turned around abruptly, heading for the door, though the route I took was somewhat hampered by the effects of the cough syrup, and I careened off a few people as I exited the place. I heard grumbles and side comments as I left, and cursed them under my breath.

When I got outside, I realized Loya had never come in with us. I looked around the porta-shitters and the sleeping huts that surrounded the MWR, and eventually found him hunched against a Hesco wall, retching once again into the dirt.

"You all right, man?" I asked.

"This was a bad idea," he said. He was right, and other people were starting to take notice of us. I walked him to a more secluded area and we both flopped down onto the ground, our bodies hitting the dirt like oversized sacks of hamburger meat. Everything had taken on a contracted quality, like a tight shot in a film that we couldn't escape, and my throat felt like a Pez dispenser every time I swallowed.

We breathed hard. "Where's Matty?" he asked.

"Matty's done, man. Some gunny snatched him up," I said. "We gotta make sure we don't head back to the hooches [tents] at the same time as him. They'll probably be tearing the place apart, looking for anything they can find." My logic seemed solid but the words felt void coming out.

Loya sighed deeply. "You know what this feels like? It feels like being drunk, but without any of the good parts." He started groaning. I told him to try to keep it down and ventured back out to see if Matty was still inside the dance. Part of me expected the MPs to already be there cuffing him and throwing him into the back of a Humvee, taking him wherever they take you when you break the law in Afghanistan.

Instead, I saw him outside of a shower hut, chatting happily with a girl who was holding a towel waiting to go in. He was peacocking hard in a real obvious way, one foot up on the steps of the showers, a hand leaning against the side. That type of approach always seemed to work for him, somehow. It was like he embodied the stereotype of a New Jersey bro so fully and with such earnestness that it became endearing. Caricatures could be real, I decided.

I called out to him, "Yo, Matty. What the fuck happened?"

He turned to me and smiled, then introduced the young corporal he was talking to. "She's intel, bro," he said. "That means she's gonna be calling in drone strikes on our AO," our area of operations. The girl seemed shy about this, as if the fact that she helped orchestrate targeted killings from a computer desk was just something she had fallen into.

"I wanted to be infantry when I enlisted," she said. Matty smirked, then started going on about how it was really time the Marine Corps let women serve in the infantry, "seeing as they had already started letting gays in and all." Sensing that the situation was under control, I went back to check on Loya.

He was standing now, looking out at the world as if he'd seen enough. "Picture the mixture, man. Picture the fucking mixture," he said with the voice of a man three times his age. Eventually Matty came and found us. I asked him what happened with the gunny and he said they had had a very civil conversation and that, after the gunny informed him that he was not dressed in appropriate attire to be in the MWR, Matty apologized sincerely and wished him a good night. *Unbelievable*, I thought. Loya and I could barely stand up straight and he had successfully dodged a potential court-martial.

"That place was a shit show, anyway. I tried to get that Wookiee's room number but she was all weird about it. A real fucking motard, she was," he said, shaking his head with distaste. Then, with a sort of Merry Prankster attitude, he made a suggestion. "Yo, what if we just raped someone? Like just said fuck it and straight raped one of these girls." He laughed as if it was the silliest thing that had ever popped into his head.

"Dude," Loya said, exhaling deeply.

"I'm just fucking around. I wouldn't actually do that." Matty tilted his head slightly. "But that would be crazy if we did."

My guess was that we were all at a point where the rules no longer seemed to apply, or, at the least, they were being significantly glossed over. When you're twenty and at war you feel entitled to just about anything. It didn't matter that we signed the contract and made the decision to be there in the first place; an act as trivial as signing a stack of paper could never legitimize what we were about to go through. And anyway, our recruiters had lied to us, or we were high when we enlisted, or we needed money for college, or we wanted to be punished for being disgusting teenage dirtbags. Or 9/11.

Matty pulled out another bottle of cough syrup from somewhere and held it up to the night sky. "Fuck you, America," he said, before chugging it down. Eventually we went back to our tent and watched a movie on Loya's laptop.

CHAPTER 5

Standard Operating Procedures

We saw a UFO that first night. The operation had just started, and we were in someone's house, a large rectangular mud compound with an open area in the center, and several small rooms at the corners that were covered with mud bricks. In the open area there seemed to be a chicken coop, judging from the clucks coming from that general vicinity. It was so dark it was hard to get a sense of things. It didn't feel like someone's house we were in, because we were half-asleep and it was a war and we referred to the locals' houses as "compounds."

Everything was fucked up and disorganized. Our convoy had hit an IED, or improvised explosive device, on the way to the village, and the guy leading the convoy had jumped out of his mine roller laughing with both of his ears bleeding. He was ecstatic. It was his third IED blast and second concussion and he was confident he would be medically discharged because of it. If you get medically discharged from the military the benefits are huge; they give you an enormous monthly compensation and you can basically chill for the rest of your life. The other guys tried to quiet him down so he wouldn't wake up the entire village, and as we sat there waiting for another mine roller to arrive, I would occasionally hear a rising whine that would turn into a hearty laugh, followed by a more accusatory tone.

"You don't get it, motherfuckers!" he was saying. "I'm done-skees. I'm going home!"

"Yeah, we know, motherfucker," they said in a hushed tone. "Just keep it down."

At night things took on a strange religious feeling. It had partly to do with the prayers being wailed from the local mosque in the village, which sounded like lost moans passing through an ancient megaphone, but it was also because of the paradox of stumbling around clumsily in the moonlight. In daylight, the command made it very clear we were patrolling an active minefield, and they had us use every SOP (standard operating procedure) imaginable— sweepers, blast diapers, avoid chokepoints and tree lines, look for command wires, etc.—whereas at night the SOPs went out the window; we could barely make out the terrain, let alone if we were standing on top of a ten-pound IED. It was an act of letting go, accepting that if we were to go up in a cloud of dirt and debris, limbs splitting off into bony fragments of fleshy mush, then the absence of vision might be a blessing.

When we got to the compound we would be living in for the next seven months, the platoon sergeant knocked on the door till a man came and opened it, staring at the group of men with rifles and body armor outside his house. Peeking out next to him were some children, and I could see a woman in a burka moving around nervously behind them. Our translator told them they had to pack up and go, that we would be living in their house for the foreseeable future. This was met with virtually no response from the man, who told his kids to start packing. The translator turned to the platoon sergeant and asked for the compensation money we were supposed to give the family. He fumbled around in his pack for a while, then called out to the lieutenant, who said he thought the sergeant had the money. There was some bickering and eventually they told the guy that he would have to come back tomorrow to get it.

The rest of us started filling sandbags in what looked like a vegetable garden that took up most of the open area of the house, tearing apart and revamping the family's home to make it military grade and as defensible from Taliban rockets as possible. We made a chain, loading the sandbags onto the tops of the rooms at the corners where four guard posts would later be erected. Someone started singing a slave song while we pitched our e-tools into the dirt, and Klesmith, a skinny kid from Philadelphia, looked up and pointed to the night sky.

"Check it out. What the fuck is that?" Everyone stopped and looked up at the white luminous orb floating high above us. They all contended it was a UFO, come to watch us wreak havoc on the people of Afghanistan. I took out my camera, a military-issued Canon XF100, and flipped a switch that put it on night vision. In the viewfinder it just looked like a green ball against a black backdrop, and the full stupidity of the war, the negligence, the absurdity, the deluded simplicity of a thing that I had assumed would be so complicated, hit me with unadulterated lucidity.

Klesmith saw me recording and began to narrate. "Here we are in Sangin, Af-derka-stan, in what is soon to be PB Watson, a shitty mud hut with no power or water, and we've just spotted what appears to be a no-shit UFO." I panned down from the green ball in the sky and zoomed in on his face, green and sickly look-ing in the night vision, with pupils lit up like a deer's crossing through headlights. "Woah, are you recording me? I didn't give my consent."

I put down the camera and looked around at the others. I no-ticed them eyeing me back. I had just gotten attached to Alpha Company that very night for the beginning of the push, and my presence aroused suspicion. As I helped them fill sandbags they would occasionally stop, look at me, and say, "Wait. Who the fuck are you?"

"Combat Camera," I'd say, embarrassed, with nothing else to add.

"We have Combat Camera with us?" and it would spread like a ripple in the dark to the others. "Hey, Combat *fucking* Camera is here."

It was my first time with the infantry and I was surprised by how skinny and malnourished they all looked. I had them pictured as muscle-bound freaks, but between all their field exercises and deployments, gym time had been replaced by long, sweaty days sheathed in about sixty pounds of ammo and flak. Muscle Milk and heaps of grilled chicken were replaced by Meals, Ready to Eat (MREs) so full of preservatives they'd stop you up for a week. In garrison, the infantry slept in their own barracks, ate at their own chow hall, and generally lived by their own rules. They did not trust POGs such as myself. POGs got people killed.

For my part, I had tried to get as much info on the operation before it started as I could, but no one knew anything, and the peo-ple who did wouldn't tell me. When I went to the company first sergeant, he laughed at me.

"It's not a push," he kept saying.

"Aye, First Sergeant," I said. He had a lazy eye that made him even more intimidating because you didn't know whether he was looking at you or something else. "What, uh . . . what would you call it, then?"

"I don't fucking know, but it ain't no push. Marjah was a push. This ain't Marjah."

"So . . ."

"It's a clear-and-hold operation."

"To clear what?" I asked.

"The fuck do you think?" he said, looking at me like I was un-fathomably dumb. "The Taliban."

"No, I mean . . ." Then he all but knocked me over, pushing me aside.

"You know," he said with his good eye cocked at me, "I could teach a fuckin' monkey to do your job."

And he left me standing there like that.

Loya said that the lack of transparency was pretty par for the course. "Usually you can find out more about the op from people back home," he told me. "In Marjah, we just listened to the news about what we were doing, and asked our parents and stuff."

"How are we supposed to report on what's going on, then?" I wondered.

Loya was a good friend but not exactly the greatest at his job. On his last deployment not a single one of his photos ever got submitted to the command for release to the public. He said it was a problem with comms—the battle for Marjah had critically damaged the means to get imagery back to the Forward Operating Bases—and the fact that the unit he accompanied had halted his work after they took too many casualties. But I think it was more to do with the fact that he enjoyed playing grunt—it's not that he was a bad photographer (on the contrary, he took vibrant pictures that captured a kind of adolescent insanity, and he knew *what* to film, too); it's just that Loya was a jock in high school. He was naturally adept at being "one of the guys." The grunts responded to that and provided enough positive reinforcement that he stopped caring about his real job, the documentary work, and instead focused on socializing with them. (I, on the other hand, was a less successful schmoozer.)

Klesmith and the rest of them had gotten over the initial shock that my presence was causing and were looking back up at the orb in the sky. Eventually the platoon sergeant came over and asked what the fuck we were doing, why everyone had stopped digging. Klesmith explained that there was a UFO, and the sergeant looked up and shook his head. "That's a flare, you retards." We went back to filling sandbags.

Alpha Company, much like the other companies in the battalion, were a group of disgruntled man-children. Most of them had been on multiple deployments and were pissed off about life in the Marine Corps, not happy to be back in Helmand for the second, third, or even fourth time. There was one guy in particular who I instinctively stayed away from. He couldn't have been more than twenty-three, but looked well over thirty. He had done a tour in Iraq and at least one in Afghanistan, yet after nearly four years in he was still an E-3. His receding hair, permanent hunch, chain-smoking, and persistent line of complaint gave him the vibe of a spiraling, middle-aged father. He kept new joins— "boots," as we called them—in a state of permanent mind-fuckery. Sometimes when they fucked up, he'd make them stand post for eighteen hours on end; other times he'd have them dig fighting holes, then do push-ups in the holes wearing their full combat load. One time I heard he tied a boot to a generator and forgot about him for a whole night. It's not that he enjoyed hazing them, but that he'd taken on the burden of educating them as a result of the Marines he'd seen get wasted before. It was an attempt to make sense of how things worked in war. If you could pinpoint what mistake led to someone's death, then you could focus on avoiding it in the future, and not have to face the randomness of our fucked-up reality. I worried about the guy's future and his kids' futures, because if he was this angry now it meant that the worst was yet to come.

In the morning there were kittens. The family was gone—they had slipped out with their stuff while we were fortifying the place, because to even be seen cooperating with us was a death warrant from the Taliban—and we realized that we were in a pretty nice hut. There were more rooms than we had thought, some complete with pillows and blankets that they'd left, an elevated level of the compound for cooking that had a large fire pit in the center, and a tool shed with wooden ladders and other things that we could use. The place even had an underground shelter that the family had built to protect them from our air strikes. Sangin, the area we were in, had been occupied by the British Army a few years back, before they had abandoned it after taking too many casualties, another section of the country that was continuously left and then reoccupied in order to keep the numbers up, maintaining the illusion of stability. So the place was still battle fresh, on both sides; almost everywhere you went there were Taliban bunkers and murder holes left over from their time with the Brits.

Klesmith was the first one to spot the litter of kittens under a stack of hay in the vegetable garden. The mother cat had probably abandoned them, too many other things to worry about. Some of the Marines took them out and started playing with them, petting them aggressively in the early morning haze. It was a perfect photo opportunity, I thought, the kind of stuff Walsh would cream himself over; Marines showing their softer side while at war. I began filming. One guy put a kitten in his cargo pocket while he walked around the compound, claiming it as the platoon's new mascot. I zoomed into the dark hole to get a shot of its beady eyes looking out from the camouflaged trousers. It was all reminiscent of past wars, heavily edited photography books of soldiers "passing time," "keeping morale high" while the bombs and guns boomed off camera.

When the hunched guy with the receding hairline saw me filming, he picked up a shovel and told Klesmith to pitch in one of the kittens.

Everyone laughed. "Yeah, that would be great for hearts and minds," someone said.

"Fuck hearts and minds," he said. "Come on, dude, pitch it in. Combat Camera can get a picture." Klesmith stood there looking at the kitten in his hand, the shovel, and then at me. At first I got the impression that they were just fucking around. But then I saw the look in some of their eyes, the leading smiles, the posturing of their young and assured bodies. Now that the idea had been presented, it was too late to go back. This would not only set the tempo for the rest of the deployment, the death and killing that would inevitably come; it would also determine my role in all of it. They would choose whether to impress the camera, including it in their war shenanigans, inevitably shaping their combat experience, or expel it, and me, from their ranks.

I continued to stand there awkwardly with my camera pointed at Klesmith, who now looked even more nervous than me, the kitten grasped tentatively in his hands as if he were in a life-or-death egg toss competition. The shovel guy would do it, we both knew that; it was up to Klesmith whether to throw it or not.

I decided to do us both the courtesy. "If you do it, I'm gonna film it and send it to your girlfriends," I said, sounding like a kid who was trying to sound like a different kid. After a pause that contained elements of disbelief and vexation, the guy with the shovel shook his head. For a second, I thought he might have shot me if he'd had his rifle on him.

"Fucking Combat Camera," he spat, dropping the shovel. He stormed off, going through the compound telling everyone I was a snitch, and once the platoon sergeant heard about my adventure in animal rights, they put me on the next convoy to Bravo, a different company that might extend me a little more tolerance.

On the ride out I was full of indignation. We'd all seen the infamous video of a puppy being thrown off a cliff that surfaced from Iraq onto YouTube in 2008, followed by an official warning from higher-ups of what not to do, or at least not to film, while at war. But I had grown up with cats. I wasn't ready for that sort of abandonment of my former self; it was too early in the deployment.

Still, the rejection was palpable, and I was left wondering what my place was in the grand scheme of the operation, if I even had one. Machine gunners machine-gunned people, artillery blew people up; even intel Marines, who were largely considered useless due to the fact that they were wrong about almost everything, contributed to the cause through the sheer title of their job. If I died, no one would give a shit because I was just some kid with a camera. My only real purpose was to get them in trouble.

After that, I decided I couldn't be the one to stop them from doing anything like that again for the rest of the deployment, no matter how fucked up things got. I would no longer be the judge and jury, but the camera still could be. I would be there filming, if they allowed it, through it all. And there would be much more killing to come. As I sat in a Mine-Resistant Ambush-Protected truck, moving like a death box through the village that was now our "area of operations," on to the next mud hut that was occupied by another group of boys with shovels and guns, I hoped that word wouldn't spread about what had happened.

CHAPTER 6

One Shot

A few weeks later I was walking up the back side of a hill with the Scout Sniper platoon. Matty had convinced them to let me tag along and film them schwack somebody. The kitten incident with Alpha Company had gone unnoticed by the rest of the battalion, most likely because they were all so spread out from each other across the AO that scuttlebutt could only get passed through the mobile platoon that resupplied each patrol base.

The snipers had taken contact the day before at the same exact spot we were now heading, and as we ascended the hill there were spent shells littered all over the ground. No one stopped to think if it was a wise idea to go back to the same place where their cover had been blown the day before, and I didn't dare question their logic. Snipers had their own way of thinking, special tactics that they learned at the grueling, three-month-long Scout Sniper School in Camp Lejeune, North Carolina. They were combat hunters, both glorified and revered, while the rest of the infantry were mere grunts.

All I knew, or thought I knew, was that they taught them how to drink their own pee when they had to stay hidden in the same position for days. Still, I was excited at the possibility of getting shot at for the first time, or filming them take someone out. Sergeant Warren, the lead sniper in charge of the squad, was a soft-spoken man who assured me before we left that something was bound to pop off. On his CamelBak he had a Nazi SS patch, the unofficial insignia of Marine *Scout Snipers*. They saw it less as a political/racial statement, I think, than as a "fuck you" to the Marine Corps' rules and regulations. It was a sniper tradition, and a sign of exclusivity that they were able to get away with it. (But it was also probably a racial statement as well.)

We took up position on the hilltop, creeping up to the edge where the Sangin Valley dropped out beneath us like a green sea trapped between desert peaks. The snipers told me to stay down so as not to be seen by any of the villagers below. I attempted to film them awkwardly while walking in a crouch, my M16 dangling around my legs, scraping along the ground like the dead weight that it was. The thing would collect dirt for most of my deployment, fired just once my entire time in Afghanistan. As they got closer to the drop-off point of the hill, they started to crawl on all fours, Warren dragging the large sack that contained his M40-A5 bolt-action sniper rifle behind him after each foot or so. It looked like a guitar case, and I didn't realize what was in it until after they'd gotten set up in the prone, and he zipped it open and started sighting in on the swath of cornfields and mud huts beneath us. His spotter, Corporal Kennelly, lay next to him looking through some binoculars.

Below us the locals ambled through the fields like ants, oblivious to our activity, tending to their crops or plotting to kill us—one was not easily discernible from the other, and, at this early stage in the deployment, not having communicated with any of them besides the few who we paid off to take over their houses, they might as well have all been Taliban. Kennelly and Sergeant Warren began to relay distance, windage, direction, etc. They had been observing from this position for a couple of weeks now since the op started, spying on the locals, studying them like killer anthropologists. I had no clue what they were looking for and, after being in the Marines for almost three years, it began to dawn on me how limited my understanding of military tactics actually was. All I knew was that I needed to keep the focus on Warren. The kill shot was the one thing I couldn't miss.

It's funny how reality and camera sometimes have an uncanny way of coexisting, complementing one another as if it were all scripted. After the squad had set up, the radioman leaned over to me and started commentating, pointing out what compounds they were looking at—"they usually have meetings over there, between the tree lines"—even telling me where to get the best shots and angles. It was like a joint production. From my position lying down I was able to pan from him back over to Warren and Kennelly, then down to the fields below. A self-contained microcosm of war was established in my head, and I could envision the end product as it was unfolding in real time; how it would be edited, the pacing and the style, even the music to go along with it. All that needed to happen now was for them to take the shot. It felt good not to be making puff pieces for AFN. This was war, for real. This was men killing men.

Two hours later, I began to worry that there might not be enough space on my camera to keep recording. It was almost full already; I had been holding on a tight shot of Warren poised, silent, and motionless for about an hour, afraid he would take the shot the second I stopped recording. Occasionally I drifted off to get some b-roll of the rest of the squad, as well as a stray dog that came walking by, staring at us curiously. I lay in the dirt, my belly resting inside my cocoon of armor and flak. A cool breeze here and there, mixed with the dual tinge of adrenaline and boredom, would bring on a childhood memory of backpacking through Yellowstone with my dad. I was about twelve years old then, and we were with a couple of my school friends and their dads. Frank Butler, the leader of the group, who had organized the trip, was a gigantic outdoorsy type with a baritone voice. I flashed back to the night my dad and Frank nearly came to blows over steak. Frank contended that our early ancestors had first started cooking meat for health reasons, early *Homo sapiens*' logical response to whatever they understood of foodborne illness. My dad argued that it was simply because cooked meat tasted better. They had been drinking wine that Frank had brought in a bota bag, and the light from the fire flickered off their reddened faces. There was no resolution to the argument, as neither side could be proven, and eventually they had to be separated. They didn't speak for the rest of the trip.

The air in Sangin felt the same as it did in Yellowstone, us kids waiting with voyeuristic horror to see how far our dads' shouting would escalate. I wondered why guys were always complaining about the heat in Afghanistan; to me it felt fine.

My thoughts wandered some more, and before I knew what was happening Warren took the shot. I flinched, causing the camera to jerk and miss the close-up I had of him, as the long-range projectile echoed through the valley.

"Fuck," Warren said, racking the bolt back and putting another round into the chamber.

"He's up and moving east," Kennelly said. Warren sighted back in. A few tense seconds passed and he fired off another shot. This time I didn't flinch.

"That one got him," Warren said.

"Not sure," said Kennelly. "He might've staggered off behind the compound. You definitely wounded him, though."

Marine snipers weren't supposed to miss. Warren put down the rifle and looked over at me self-consciously. They definitely weren't supposed to fire multiple shots after an enemy combatant was incapacitated or unable to fight back.

It wasn't till a week later that I was able to pin down Warren for an interview. Every time I approached him, he'd say he was too busy or couldn't do it that day. I started to feel like even more of a nuisance.

When he finally gave in, we went over to a side post of their patrol base to set up, where an Afghan soldier was standing guard while singing to himself. I asked him to leave for a bit, but he didn't understand. I pointed to the camera and then to Warren and motioned for him to leave, and eventually he smiled and gave me a thumbs-up.

"Afghanistan good? No good?" he asked before leaving.

"No good," I said. He agreed contritely.

I couldn't get Warren to stop talking like a robot, reciting Marine Corps textbook definitions about the mission of surveillance target acquisition teams and statistics that had no relevance to what had happened on the hilltop. I couldn't figure out why he was being so opaque, and I wondered if years of killing people through the remote intimacy of his long-range telescopic rifle had made him incapable of normal human interaction.

"So, you guys were out there to observe for Taliban activity," I said. "Can you go into what you were looking for?"

"We had gotten intel from historical firing points that there was enemy activity in the area . . . so we wanted to go and take a gander," he said in a monotone.

"Okay." I nodded vigorously to show him that I understood. This was going well. As long as he sounded professional and didn't curse or talk about "killing hajis," Walsh would probably release the video. Vagueness in military affairs was always best, but I needed at least a few sound bites that would explain what had happened so people back home could make sense of it; otherwise it would look too much like what it was, a Jarhead shooting people in a cornfield.

"All right, so the first shot," I said. "Can you walk me through—"

He cut me off. "Hey, man, can you turn off the camera real quick?"

He looked around awkwardly as I stopped recording. "We reported that it was only one shot. Can you just edit the other one out or something?"

It started to become clear. "Look," I said, "my job is to make you guys look as good as possible. I couldn't show you fucking up even if I wanted to. So, whatever you need me to do, just let me know." He relaxed a little and we went on with the interview. One of the things they teach you at the Defense Information School is to ask your interview subject if they have anything else they'd like to add at the end of the interview.

Warren thought for a minute, then delivered a real winner, very wholesome-like. "It's said that every Taliban a sniper takes out saves three Marines' lives. And saving Marines is something I take very seriously."

When I showed him and the rest of the squad the final edited video on my laptop, they stood around and watched in stoic silence. "That's a pretty high-def camera you got," Corporal Kennelly said. "The Marine Corps gave you that?"

Walsh was quick to release it to DVIDS after I burned the video to a disk and got it on a chopper to Leatherneck. A few days later it ended up on YouTube under the title "ONE SHOT ONE KILL, MARINE SNIPER TAKES OUT TALIBAN FIGHTER." That video has 16 million views now. In the comments section a separate war wages between the trolls and would-be jihadists.

"COUNTER TERRORISTS WIN"

"One less raghead."

"AMERICAN SCUM"

""ستموت بنعمة الله""

"I wanted to see the guy get shot! Lame ass video . . ."

"One dead Talib saves three marines lives? What a fat head. If you weren't there killing you have no threat of being killed."

"YOU WILL BE THE NEXT FUCKER TO GET IT"

"are those Nazi SS runes on the dude's camelback?"

From then on, my nickname was "YouTube." Loya was "Facebook," because he took photos mostly. Guys wanted us around now, hoping to be the next big internet sensation, or at least have something to show for their time at war. Also around that time, in our heads, the movie began to form; a secret movie, the brainchild of Loya and me. The war movie to end all war movies. The characters would be the grunts. If we could get it right, it would be so mind-shatteringly raw, so crazy, that there wouldn't be the need for any more *Hurt Locker*s or *American Snipers*, movies that would feel like Super Bowl half-time ads compared to what we were going to do.

We would aim for making the *Kids* of the modern war era. Larry Clark's 1995 taboo classic about youth gone rotten in New York City during the end of the AIDS crisis was, after all, a war movie in certain ways, in that the streets were a battleground of sex, drugs, and violence. And just like those Vietnam antiwar movies of yesteryear, originally intended as cautionary tales about the folly and horror of war, but that had become more successful at getting young men to enlist than *Call of Duty*, *Kids* had become an anthem of teenage not-giving-a-fuckness. Movement, sweat, spit, and blood. Broken skulls on the pavement from skateboard cracks to the head and forced laughter at lewd jokes. Performance, humiliation. Victory through sex and making it through to the end of the night as one party unfurls into another like battle scenes in *Apocalypse Now*. Shot guerrilla-style, the movie *Kids* channeled the actual rhythm and language of adolescence in such a way that it couldn't help but titillate; it didn't moralize and it didn't front. The kids in the movie weren't even real actors, at least not at the time. They were just kids.

And so were we, but with guns.

What people didn't understand about our wars was that they weren't run by the politicians or generals, or even the defense contractors or corporations. They were run by eighteen to twenty-three-year-old kids without college degrees and little on their minds besides getting some trigger time. Sure, big money might be funding the whole operation, but they didn't have a clue about what was happening inside it all, the way we lived, the weight that had been entrusted to us. And in the same sense that the characters in *Kids* ran untethered through the streets of New York, kings of their stoops and subways and parks, we were kings of our war, emperors of our wadis, sultans of our mud huts.

Afghanistan set us free, free from the stress of figuring out what we would do with the rest of our lives (survival was the most immediate concern), free from the internet and our parents and girlfriends, and, of course, free from the bullshit that we had to endure while in garrison—the mindless training, the constant cleaning, the asinine orders and regulations. It was almost silly to think about—TOW missiles that cost $15,000 a pop, JDAMs and Hellfires, grenade launchers and AT-4s, machine guns and night-vision goggles. We patrolled with gear strapped to our bodies and firepower at our command that totaled more in U.S. dollars than the average college student's debt, more than the amount the government would pay to our next of kin if we died. The burden was ours, too, one that we simultaneously loathed and relished. That's what we would capture in our war movie.

There was one problem, obviously: we, Combat Camera, were propagandists. We weren't even allowed to show personnel using profanity or smoking cigarettes, let alone the frontline mayhem this film would require for authenticity. But there were ways around it; it was a war, after all. We had been given the kind of access that civilian journalists could only dream about.

Loya and I decided it was best to split up and cover more ground, more chances for blood and guts and grunt antics. Corporal Lewis, a Public Affairs Marine who held almost the same job as us, except that he wrote stories more than taking photos, looked upon us warily. He loathed the Marine Corps more than anyone I knew, but he still could be a real stickler for the job sometimes. He was the type who couldn't sleep if he had failed to meet a deadline. Not a bad guy, just very neurotic when it came to getting his work done.

"You know I'm not in charge of you guys," he said, "so I'm not gonna tell you what you can and can't do, but just be careful. Shit like this can roll downhill if you don't watch out. Last year I was showing the battalion commander some photos of a shura [meeting] that we conducted with the locals and I didn't realize the platoon I was with had taken my camera when I wasn't looking. I'm scrolling through pics of Marines giving volleyballs and shit to the Afghans, when up comes a bunch of photos of them field-fucking each other. I'm talking dicks, balls, and assholes everywhere, like inches from the camera." He took his camera and held it beneath his crotch to demonstrate. "Next thing, they're being forced to wear full PPE at all times even when they're inside the wire, standing post with two men on each watch." Lewis shook his head, still haunted by the incident. Loya and I could empathize, a combat cameraman's worst nightmare. It was one thing to get ourselves in trouble, quite another to cause problems for the guys in the unit.

There was, of course, also the problem of our audience. Guys in Vietnam used to watch John Wayne movies like *Sands of Iwo Jima* before shipping out, Marines in the Gulf War would watch *Deer Hunter* and *Full Metal Jacket*, but the millennial military was something else. The post–reality TV product of cameras being placed into every situation imaginable. There were dark subcultures of kids who genuinely got off on the extreme gore and violence available at modern fingertips 24/7, and quite a few of them wound up in the U.S. military. Columbine shooter fan clubs, LiveLeak junkies, and 4chan addicts. Full-blown 9/11 truthers who were now waging the War on Terror.

Being eighteen means being both dumber and intellectually superior to adults, impressionable and impenetrable at the same time. You can't tell an eighteen-year-old nothing, unless it happens to be something like, "Getting shot at is better than sex." They're horny yet abstinent, vile yet pure. And the videos we watched growing up opened a door to the hidden parts of reality, while also distorting it. Internet porn taught us how to fuck while heightening the act to the point of pastiche, so that when we did it for real, mimicking the words and sounds and movements, it felt less intimate, less authentic than when we were alone in our rooms in front of a screen. We weren't just desensitized, we were transubstantiated into a new design, a new frame of looking, feeling, believing. It was hard to process, and left you feeling removed from it all the more inundated you got. Things happened in videos of real life, for instance, that could not be explained; the more the world was documented, the less sense it started to make.

"Explain that shit to me," Lance Corporal Saxby, a SAW gunner, argued with me on patrol one morning, insistent that the World Trade Center could not possibly have come down due to jetliners alone. "You can see the bombs go off in the middle of the building; it's right there in the video." Saxby, or Sax as we called him, was a Black kid from Georgia with a shrill, ululating voice that made it sound like he was on constant Auto-Tune. He had real bad razor bumps across his jawline and needed a no-shave chit, but even in Afghanistan it was hard to get one from the docs due to Marine Corps regulations. In a country where the men respected you more the longer your facial hair was, we were still forced to walk around like clean-shaven babyfaces, thus alienating the locals even further from us. Sax was sighting in on a guy in a field who was stooped over, looking back at us strangely. Everyone was shady.

"And you thought this before you joined?" I asked.

"Of course. I'm not stupid."

"Huh. I'm just curious, why fight in a war if you think it's for the wrong side?"

He scoffed. "I don't give a fuck about politics. I'm out here to kill, dawg. Plain and simple." Sax wanted to kill someone. That was why he joined the Marine Corps. But just like the videos, it was more than morbid curiosity.

How to make art, then? Loya and I thought. Something new in a generation that's seen it all before, traumatized by the image before even getting to the war. Post-allegiance and post-truth. We were both film buffs; surely we could think of something unique to add cinematically.

Loya pondered this as he took a pull of some of the best hashish we'd ever smoked. I watched the smoke drift over the ledge of the abandoned machine gun nest we were in, down into the gully beneath us. We were standing at the Kajaki Dam, a hydroelectric power plant that fueled the entire Helmand River Valley. We'd been sent up there to photograph a panoramic view of the dam for some intel folks; the purpose was unclear. Unbeknownst to us at the time, the dam was actually the sole reason our unit was in Afghanistan. The "push" was a clearing operation to secure a road through Taliban-held Sangin up to Kajaki, so that seven hundred tons of cement could be safely transported to the dam, which had been in need of repair since the U.S. built it in the 1950s. Humanitarian ops, real benevolent stuff. Of course, the dam had never been completed (it was also a bombing target for the Air Force immediately after 9/11), so it was kind of our fault the thing was broken in the first place.

After we took the photos, we went exploring. The place had a magical feel to it, a history that predated the conflicts that had plagued the country, back in the days when Kabul was called the "Paris of Central Asia." The views were from another world. We could see the whole war from up there, all the hamlets and desert that our Marines were inhabiting. In the distance, two puffs of smoke from a double IED rose like chimney fumes. The earth was a war factory.

Some Afghan soldiers led us to the "Russians' last stand," their name for a torture house where a whole company of Soviet Spetsnaz were left behind and slaughtered by the mujahideen in 1989. Before the Russians invaded in 1979, it had been the living quarters for the people who worked on the dam. Now it left behind a much grislier tale. It was three stories, each floor allowing for a different mental recreation. This was some real eerie shit: bullet holes everywhere, chairs bolted to the floor. Apparently the Russians had managed to hold them back for a couple of days before running out of ammo, and when they did the mujahideen had stormed the place and flayed them alive, going floor to floor torturing the remaining soldiers. It was uncanny to see evidence of such catastrophic fatality from a superpower who was, at the time, facing the same ragtag group of fighters that we now were. It could happen to us, too; it *did* happen occasionally, in small pockets of the country that the war had forgotten about. Combat Outpost Keating, the Battle of Wanat, Korengal . . . the list went on longer than the DoD would be comfortable with you knowing.

The Afghans seemed to delight in showing us. After the tour, one of them took out a trash bag full of official Afghan National Army (ANA) track suits emblazoned with the colors of their flag. The poor bastards didn't even have a real army but they had some nice track suits; all black with a green line cutting through a black and red embossed diamond over the chest. Loya's eyes moistened with appreciation when a soldier handed one to him. "I've been trying to get one of these for years, dude. You have no idea."

I asked if they had any "charz," which always triggered an obliga-tory pageant of disbelief and skepticism from our Afghan counter-parts. "*Charz?*" they would repeat, eyes wide and innocent. Did we really think they indulged in such shameful behavior? "No, no, no," they would demand. "Charz, *no good*. Charz, *nishta*." But, of course, after some gentle persuading, the craftiest and, for some reason, always the most diminutive of the soldiers would motion for us to stay while he shuffled off and came back with more hash than we could ever have hoped for. They never accepted any money, either.

Before we left, I noticed their commander shaking his head sadly, disappointed that we, the world's greatest fighting force, sent there to lead by example and guide his soldiers to victory and democracy, displayed the same lack of discipline as his own men. I felt embarrassed then. The stakes were so much higher for him and the rest of the ANA, more than we would ever come to appreciate. They were doomed once we left; we knew it and so did they. But my guilt passed pretty quickly, as it always did, by remembering that, for us at least, it was all a show. And after all, I was just a cameraman. It's not like I was actually a part of what was happening there.

This line of thought, or lack thereof, got me by for quite a while. It actually got me through the war and out of the Marine Corps. But time always comes knocking; eventually it came for all of us, albeit in different ways. It was just a matter of when we would choose to let it in.

"One thing's for sure, we gotta put Skrillex in there."

"'Kill Everybody'?" I asked.

"Nah. 'First of the Year,'" Loya said. "The U of sound."

Loya and I had waited till nightfall to smoke and have a brain-storm sesh in a secluded old machine gun bunker we found that must have been another relic from the Russians; hard to tell, really, as with everything else about Afghanistan. It wasn't totally necessary for us to take precautions about getting high, because Marines in the field pretty much always looked stoned; dirt-grimed faces and sunken eyes, it was kind of the look. "If anyone asks if you're high, just say you're tired," Matty would instruct us. "It works because we're always tired." Out there, the hash-fueled paranoia of getting caught mingled with the fear of getting killed, and in cotton-mouthed whispers, under cover of darkness, we would assure ourselves that the Taliban wasn't crazy enough to attack at night.

Loya was always talking about something he'd coined called the "U of sound," which he'd drawn a detailed map of in his notebook that explained how sound moved and changed depending on where you were, your frame of mind. It didn't make a lot of sense to me but I knew he'd been shot at a lot and his ears were pretty damaged, so that might have had something to do with it.

"But we can't just make an hour-long moto video set to the soundtrack of our deployment. That would be lame as fuck," I said.

Eventually we came up with something we thought would be a real game changer as far as war docs went: After the tour was over, if we weren't dead or missing our legs, we would bring the camera home with us on the thirty days of deployment leave they gave us when we returned. Me and Loya off to New York to blow our combat pay on a large quantity of drugs (preferably hallucinogens), and then—and here was the real genius part— we'd splice the footage of us taking the drugs with flashbacks to Afghanistan.

In our minds it would be easy. We were Marines so we were already willing to go the extra mile. It meant seeking out the most kinetic action we could find and filming it in the most brazen ways possible. Kicking in doors shoulder to shoulder with the point men, climbing onto roofs with the designated marksmen and zooming in through their scopes, strapping GoPros to everything we could find; real gonzo shit, we thought.

It also meant getting the one thing that was so elusive in war porn: the kill shot. Not just guys squeezing off rounds (half the time they weren't even shooting at anything), but the moment of impact, the bad guy's head turning into pink mist for the camera—what was absent from my "ONE SHOT ONE KILL" video. Robert Capa's *The Falling Soldier*, Richard Drew's *The Falling Man*. Back in 2011, when we were out there (before cops started wearing body-cams), it was usually surveillance cameras that caught it or dash-cams where the moment happens slightly off-screen, anticlimactic; the death was happenstance. Google satellite photos that captured UFOs by accident. But that would not do for us. It would have to be cinematic.

We sat there stoned, imagining the heaps of awards we'd receive and praise from both the military and civilian world for capturing the "brutality of war" in such an "unvarnished" and "candid" way. "Visceral," it would be described. "Psychedelic." Our bravery would be lauded as well, for running into the fire. For never putting down the camera. "The brave ones shot bullets, the crazy ones shot film." That corny slogan from Vietnam, which were the glory days of journalism, back when you could actually make a differ-ence just by photographing a napalmed girl or an executed VC. Now there was no difference to make. Prowar, antiwar—it didn't really mean anything anymore. The ideology had exhausted its signification, faded into layers of indifferences and oh-dear-isms. The aesthetics of the documentation now mattered more than the content itself.

Loya scratched his stomach. "We should get suits, too," he said.

"What do you mean?"

"When we go to New York, we gotta buy suits. We should wear the suits on the subway when we take mushrooms."

"Shrooms and suits," I said.

"Yup. Do it in style."

CHAPTER 7

The Four Locos

I f it's a movie, it's easier. Even though the sound of gunfire is so loud it hurts not just your ears, but your stomach down into your soul, the camera eases the pain. It shrinks the world down into a tight box. It makes you home in on that viewfinder and diminishes everything else, the way a sentence omits what's left unsaid. The pieces of metal flying around you become like paper lost in the wind. The camera is an enjoiner, a call for everyone to give their all during the fight. No one wants to get caught on video looking like a pussy.

Their whoops and hollers take on new levels of meaning when they feel its presence pass over them. The unrelenting sound of an M240 machine gun nailing home the truth of the country boy's delirious song; the truth his father knew in Vietnam, and his father before him in the great battles of the unimaginable. They didn't have good cameras or portable microphones back then, so we have to rely on the tripod mechanics of toy soldier movements lost in the fuzzy reels of John Ford's fantasies. Oftentimes, when the Hollywood director was serving in the Navy as head of their

Field Photographic Division during World War II (while taking a hiatus from filming John Wayne slaughter a bunch of Jewish actors pretending to be Indians), Ford would miss a battle and then have the soldiers re-create them for stock footage that would be shown in cinemas back home. The people watching had no idea, unless they looked closely and were able to see a GI smirking in the background as Ford had them all running around pretending to outflank the enemy or storm a beach. What effect, I wonder, did these false images have on generations who grew up seeing men never flinch as they ran, robotically, toward the action?

Battle scene re-creation is a lost art now, but as Combat Camera we learned to fake other things. Our real job, after all, was not to show the war in Afghanistan. It was to show the goodwill and benevolence of our troops abroad. Anytime there was a Marine handing out a soccer ball to an Afghan kid, we'd be there filming. Anytime the Engineer Battalion was building a school, we'd be there getting interviews. Whenever there was a shura with the local elders, or the Female Engagement Teams (FETs) were talking with Afghan women about their concerns, we'd be there recording. They didn't actually have to be saying anything of substance; they just had to be in the same room moving their lips, and we could stitch together a scene of coalition forces working hand in hand with the locals to build Afghanistan up.

While the grunts were running around killing, there was a sideshow taking place, and that was useful for different periods of time. When President Barack Obama needed more troops, videos of soldiers under fire would play heavily on Fox and CNN, showing the boys taking the fight to the enemy, but when there was talk of actual withdrawal, on came the peaceful clips we made of soldiers digging wells and Civil Affairs Groups giving textbooks to little girls. What would happen to women's education if we left? What would happen to the wells? It's as if the unjustifiability of the war became a thought experiment to see how ambiguous and confusing the media could make it, testing the limits of the American ability to accept the nuances of our leaders' grand schemes, and the unstoppable force of the military-industrial complex.

Halfway through the deployment I made a video package of us building a school right in the center of the busiest bazaar in our AO. It was supposed to show how we had reclaimed the area from the Taliban and created a tiny box of democracy. They had some women teachers flown out from Kabul to take selfies with the FET, and I went around recording the kids as they all jumped and clamored around me, looking at my camera, then ran away whenever I actually tried to get a shot of them, like shy schools of fish. In that moment they looked so blissful, and I was almost able to convince myself that what we were doing had substance, and I felt proud to be documenting this aspect of the war, aside from the death and destruction that people normally expect to see. It was the White-savior Hollywood boy in me that was able to look at the small things as a microcosm for the bigger picture. No, maybe the war didn't make sense, but we made a small difference here in this village, for a moment in time.

It was a few months later that they opened the school for the first day of class. Loya and I were in our tent eating care packages when we heard the bomb, and we all stopped and waited. We groaned when we heard the approaching footsteps because we knew what that meant. We went down to film the aftermath for intel and archival purposes; this, of course, would not be released to the public. There were around thirty dead children in the blast, and amid them all was the leader of the FET, a female lieutenant who was walking around pissed off and confused, tending to her wounded Marines, so overcome with adrenaline she didn't even seem to notice that her right arm was hanging off her shoulder like a weighed-down puppet. She would have to have it amputated later that day. As morbid and fucked up as it sounds, my first thought went to the FET's Facebook page, and I wondered if she would take down the selfies of her and the kids, or if she would maybe spin it into a memento, a sacrifice of her time doing the work of educating young girls in a backward place.

Then we would film the memorials, my least favorite part of the job because they lumped everyone into Christian services, and for some reason one of the guys who had died always wanted that song "Chicken Fried" by the Zac Brown Band played at their service—"A cold beer on a Friday night, a pair of jeans that fit just right"—and I dreaded the thought that my Jew ass would get put into a Christian memorial with the Zac Brown Band playing, and they'd send the video home to my parents, who would watch flabbergasted. I almost got baptized during boot camp (it was an excuse to get out of work duty on Sundays and go to church), but my dad flipped out and talked me out of it when I wrote to him about it. What would they think if I died and all they had left was a memorial video with a Christian chaplain reading off random Bible verses?

These were things to consider as I spent my time flipping between the true, the untrue, and the inconclusive. I would film a puff piece about working with the Afghan Army and interview Lance Corporal Schmuckatelli to get a sound bite of progress and cohesion.

"The Afghan Army guys we're working with are ... uh ... pretty motivated. They want to ... it seems like they want to, you know, help their people, and ... uh ..."

"Take over after we leave," I'd whisper behind the camera.

"Take over the mission after we leave," he'd say, trying to keep a straight face.

Then I'd turn the camera off and on again and ask him what he really thought.

"I hope everyone here dies," he'd say, without missing a beat. "I don't give a fuck about the ANA or the Afghan people. They're all gay and fuck little boys. The ANA and ANCOP [Afghan National Civil Order Police] fuck each other all the time, I've seen it. Fucking disgusting. I've walked in on them a bunch of times. When they're not fucking each other, they're fucking goats out in the fields."

"What do you think about the future of Afghanistan?"

"I think we should just drop a bomb and leave."

"Do you really think that?"

"Yes. There's no point in us being here. The Taliban will come back anyway."

"What're you going to do when you get out of the Marines?"

"Buy a motorcycle."

"That's it?"

"Yep. Drive across the country."

"Thanks for your time, Lance Corporal Schmuckatelli."

———

Time did funny things while you were there. Like when the Taliban seemed to go on a sabbatical for a couple of months and we were left to play war in our heads. The need for movies was strongest then. I was with Third Platoon, or Turd Platoon as they liked being referred to, by far the most belligerent group of Marines I had ever seen. It was like they were a theater troupe of psychopaths. Tony, Rodriguez, Valdez, and Klasko; they called themselves the "Four Locos," named after the recently banned alcoholic energy drink, Four Loko, which was notorious for causing intense blackouts. One day we were on patrol and Tony beckoned for a kid to come over by holding out a piece of chocolate from an MRE. When the kid got to him, Tony picked him up and threw him into a wadi that was about six feet deep full of shit water. Tony turned to the camera afterward and held up four fingers, and Rodriguez came into the shot as well to pose with him. The other children laughed like it was the funniest thing they'd ever seen, while the kid in the wadi climbed out of the water sobbing. When he got out, he sat there all wet and mopey, but after a few minutes he started to crack a smile. The kids were tough as nails and we treated them as such, pelting them with rocks when they wouldn't leave us alone, giving them rigged MRE heating pouches that would go off in their hands. It seemed like Turd Platoon wanted to see how far they could take it, and one day Tony pulled a pistol on a group of boys riding by on donkeys. "WHERE'S THE TALIBAN?! WHERE'S THE FUCKING TALIBAN?!" he screamed like a mental patient. It was a question that, at that point, we were all asking ourselves; we hadn't been shot at in so long that we were starting to worry about them, like a relative you hadn't heard from in a while.

It didn't bother me so much when Tony fucked with the kids, but my stomach turned sour when he did it to the elders. We would set up a vehicle checkpoint and he'd motion for a guy on a moped to stop, then he'd start whacking him gleefully with a stick like a dominatrix, really getting into it, the country his stage, the people his props. Sometimes the locals served as nothing but a form of our amusement, and when Tony was unleashed there was no low that he wouldn't stoop to. An ugly, brash Virginia boy with a missing tooth, he had steroids shipped out to the PB from Japan that would give him vicious mood swings. Perhaps that partly explained it, but I think mostly he just hated himself.

Once, we were sent out to a crossing in the Helmand River to set up a surveillance outpost and observe for the Taliban moving weapons. We took over a compound occupied by a single old man, a little girl, and two young boys. The place was bleak. I wasn't sure what they were subsisting on. The old guy was too feeble to farm, and the kids were too small to do much, either. The area surrounding their house was strange and barren, beautiful no doubt, with the river just a skip away and large cliffs jutting up in the distance, but as far as living went it seemed like an unfinished idea. There weren't any crops nearby except for a dying marijuana field, and out by the cliffs there were some Jogi milling around, Afghan gypsies who rode on horses and lived in large tents. Like so many parts of the country, it made you wonder what was really going on; if there was a secret underneath, other than what we just assumed, which was that they were all working for the Taliban. Something deeper that spoke of ancient thoughts and dreams. It felt like a video game when you'd take the map to its limit and hit the big glitch, and the earth would drop out into an endless white void where you could see parts of places that were built but then forgotten by the game's designers.

We told the old guy he had to pack up and leave while we lived in his compound for the next week or so. For some reason, we hadn't bothered to bring an interpreter (I think whatever intel we'd gotten had said that the place was uninhabited, or maybe we'd just shown up at the wrong house), but the man seemed to understand. Slowly, he and his children started to gather their things. The little girl wouldn't stop staring at me, a filthy stuffed elephant clutched tightly in her arms. I took out my camera and flipped the viewfinder around so she could take a look at herself, something that usually made the kids go wild, but she didn't even smile, just continued to stare at me with eyes like stone.

The rest of the Four Locos were on the roof, shirtless, arguing about who would stand post first. Klasko consented after Corporal Valdez, the squad leader, half-heartedly threatened to pull rank, and he grudgingly set up his 240 atop a few sandbags, pointed it in the direction of the mountains, plopped his large body down, and began packing an emptied cigarette with hash.

Tony called to him from the other side of the roof. "You smoke that shit too much, man. That's why you're a fat-body, getting the munchies all the time. You need to get svelte, like me." He started flexing, tensing every muscle and nerve in his body till the veins in his face were jutting out, then, like an engine releasing excess steam, he brayed, "See?! See?! See?!" repeatedly through his teeth.

Klasko didn't even bother looking up from his lap, where he was rolling the joint, and said, "Yeah, well, at least I don't jerk off in front of the mirror." The truth of this statement stung Tony, and he sat down on the roof despondently, looking out across the fields.

I lay in the open area of the compound, where the sun was coming through a hole in the clouds, and watched the old man carry some pillows into a wheelbarrow. I debated lazily whether I should film him, and maybe try to piece together some kind of story for Walsh. I hadn't produced a video package in weeks, ever since I got to Third. Although they were true camera whores who wanted me to film them doing any and everything (working out, smoking hash, interviews where they would rail against their company first sergeant, who they claimed was withholding weights, protein shakes, cereal, and other goodies they believed they were entitled to, simply because he disliked them. "He just hates us 'cause we have the most NJPs [nonjudicial punishments] in the battalion. If he doesn't like doing paperwork, he shouldn't be the fucking first sergeant"), nothing they did was releasable by Marine Corps Public Affairs standards. For one, they never wore proper PPE—most of the time Tony didn't even wear a helmet, opting instead for an American flag bandana—and two, they were unhinged. An average patrol with them would spark outrage among people back home.

I tried to imagine what a video package of Third Platoon would look like. "Today, Marines with Third Platoon, Bravo Company, of the First Battalion, Sixth Marine Regiment, in joint cooperation with Afghan forces, brought local residents of Sangin together to view something that had been withheld from them by the Taliban for decades: porn. It all began as part of a humanitarian operation to win the hearts and minds of the weary residents of Helmand Province. While handing out coloring books and candy to the local children, one of them asked Lance Corporal Klasko, of Sacramento, California, what the strange device in his hand was, an iPhone. Lance Corporal Rodriguez, of Fredericksburg, Texas, suggested to Lance Corporal Klasko that he show the young boy a video that was saved in his library. When it was revealed to the boy that said video was a gang bang, shock waves were sent out across the land, as local elders and villagers from the surrounding area came running to see the graphic content. In no time at all, a mob had formed, with people pushing and clambering to get a view. It's these types of bonding moments between Marines and Afghan nationals that contribute to the counterinsurgency mission in more ways than are imaginable. . . ."

The closest to any semblance of professionalism I'd filmed them display was on a bunker demolition mission they'd conducted. Since no one was shooting at us, we were able to walk freely through the AO and destroy all the bunkers the Taliban had built. Hession, a combat engineer, would crawl inside the tiny mud fortifications and lace them with C4 explosives. I'd set up the camera on the ground, and Valdez and Klasko would stand in front of the bunker waiting for Hession to pop smoke, then they'd start walking toward the camera like badasses, so that afterward I could edit it to make it seem like it blew up just as they were walking past me, even though there was still a minute left before detonation.

During one of these demolitions, the Taliban tried to be slick and plant an IED in one of the bunkers in anticipation of us going inside it. The plan backfired, however, when the IED went off while the guy was setting it up. Valdez and Rodriguez were rap battling when we heard the explosion and went over to inspect. The guy was in pieces, strung about in a tree next to the now-destroyed bunker.

"He blew it for us! That was nice of him," Tony said. The only thing we could find that was still intact was one of his hands, and I could have made a real banger of a propaganda piece, showing how the Taliban were getting desperate and weren't even properly trained enough to successfully plant the homemade bombs they made (score one for America), had they not picked up the dude's severed hand and started chasing me around with it anytime I tried to get a shot.

They were most definitely unhinged, and I could see them being the next Maywand District if the right cards fell into place. The important thing about Maywand, the site of a string of civilian murders in 2009 by a platoon of soldiers who called themselves the "Kill Team," was that the unit hadn't taken contact once the entire time they'd been there leading up to the murders. The place was more peaceful than a sleepy suburb in the States; zero Taliban activity. They actually had to frag themselves before they shot the civilians so that they could call it in as an attack. When I looked at the photos of them smiling, holding the dead Afghans by the backs of their heads as if they were prize bucks, I couldn't help but think about the camera. Why were we always filming the things we shouldn't be doing? The souvenir aspect of war tourism for the young and depraved of American society. Proof of the cool factor. Would the torture at Abu Ghraib prison in Iraq have happened if they didn't have a camcorder? Maybe I was overestimating my own relevance, but it still made you wonder about the performance of it all. If we didn't have cameras we'd just *be* there, instead of one step removed, the necessary distance for us to really milk it.

The old man was loading some yellow jugs full of gasoline or some other liquid into the wheelbarrow now, and I decided to get up and try to make the girl smile. I gave her a marble pound cake from my MRE, but she just took it and gave it to her brothers. I tried snapping a chem light and waving it in front of her, but she didn't even break eye contact with me to look at it. I was about to give up and go lie back in the sun when I saw a rock come soaring off the roof and hit the old man on the back while he was stooped over. He straightened up slowly and looked around, confused. Tony was lying on his side like a teenage girl on a beach, looking down at the guy with a bored expression on his face. The old man went back to what he was doing. Another rock came down and landed on his turban. And another. He was ignoring them now and continued to move his things. Inside I pleaded with Tony to stop. *For the love of God, please stop.* I walked toward the man, thinking that if I stood near him I might be able to deflect attention, but Tony didn't seem to notice. It almost looked as though he wasn't even conscious of what he was doing, as if he were skipping stones into the sea while daydreaming about a lost love. I looked around at the others. They were already too stoned to give a shit, and probably wouldn't have said anything anyway. I was stuck between the sickness of watching and the knowledge that if I intervened, I might not be able to film him again, or he might not feel comfortable doing the things he did so naturally. At that point in the deployment, Tony was one of my stars; he'd given me good material. Nothing I would be willing to show anyone for years to come, of course, but still essential to the scumbag diaries I was half-consciously chronicling, a section perhaps titled "Downtime." It was all fun and games, you see. There were things he did that *were* actually funny, like that time he sprayed a bunch of kids with silly string, or did push-ups with them on his back.

The little girl continued to stare at me. I led her to another part of the compound and sat with her for a while, the old man in my periphery still getting softly pelted with rocks. As I looked at her, I felt my eyes glazing over, until we were both stone figures in a staring contest and the mud walls around us were a sanctuary of childhood detachment. In that moment I knew that she would never forget us; forever she would remember the shirtless men who took over her house and threw rocks at her grandfather. Eventually her gaze slipped away from mine, her thoughts drifting to another place, but I tried to convince myself that we had had a moment of silent recognition. In reality, she probably thought I was some kind of psychopath.

When we lay down for the night, after the old man and kids had left, I hoped with everything in my heart that we'd get shot at soon.

———

"How you doing, man?"

Lewis had found me alone in my mud hut, laptop plugged into a generator, going through the footage for the hundredth time. Matteucci, the squad druggie, had just scored some opium on patrol and we'd smoked it through a Pringles can salvaged from a care package. I could barely keep my eyes open. He'd managed to amble onto post afterward, but I was feeling pretty heavy, and when Lewis parted the poncho liner that was hanging over the entrance to my room, he took one look at me and got concerned.

"You good?"

I scratched my head and looked around my domicile. Light was coming through a smoke hole in the ceiling and dust particles floated around in the shimmer. We both laughed. "Yeah, man. What brings you out here?"

"S-3 is doing a swap with us. You're going down to Weapons Company, Loya's getting sent to Alpha, and I'm gonna be here with Bravo. You didn't hear?"

My heart sank. "What? No. Why are they doing that? That doesn't make any sense."

"When has anything this battalion's done ever made sense?"

I shook my head and looked down at my laptop. "I can't leave here, man. I . . . you don't understand. I built rapport with these guys."

"This isn't coming from me, dude. It's coming from the top. Also, it probably wouldn't hurt for you to get somewhere with SIPRNet and check your email. Chief Warrant Officer Walsh has been hitting up my CO, Colonel Wright, who's been hitting me up asking why you and Loya haven't submitted anything lately."

I just stared at him. "What?"

"Look, man, get your fuckin' shit together. Mobile's waiting to take you down to Weapons."

He was growing intolerant of me, I could tell. I got up slowly and started packing my ruck. "It's not like it matters," I said. "There's not shit happening in this whole fucking AO."

"Well, we still have a job to do. And anyway, you just want footage for your stupid movie. Don't be such a fucking tourist, man. You should feel lucky no one's getting hurt."

I scoffed, but inside I knew he was right. I said good-bye to the guys. Some of them were upset to see me go, others not so much. The camera legitimized but also distracted them; it could lead to bad things if not viewed with the proper dose of skepticism.

"We didn't even get into a tick for you, man!" Tony lamented.

"Watch us take contact the minute you leave." Before I left, he made me burn him a disk of all the footage I had of his antics, so that one day he could show his kids "what it was like out here." I couldn't imagine why he would want them to see what an asshole he was, but I admired his commitment to posterity.

CHAPTER 8

Theater of War

I was in a sour mood during the whole convoy ride. When I got to the new PB it was too dark to see anything, and I just set up my sleeping mat on the ground somewhere where no one would step on me and passed out. In the morning I was having a dream about rockets hitting our position that turned out not to be a dream and I woke up with a guy on the post above me screaming, "RPG! That was a fucking RPG! Holy shit, it went right over my head!"

Mortars started erupting nearby and everything came alive very quickly. I grabbed my camera and ran outside the compound, where guys were lighting up a cliff wall about five hundred meters across the river. Tracers were flying through the air. I realized I was wearing flip-flops and that it would be stupid if I died wearing flip-flops, and ran back inside to put on boots.

"See the fucking square?!" the platoon commander screamed at one of their SAW gunners. "Shoot the fucking square!!" They were all running around like monkeys who'd just been released from a petting zoo. You could tell they hadn't taken contact in a long, long time; this was a special treat for them. A kid manning a turret gun in one of their trucks was laughing hysterically as he sent .50-cal rounds in the same direction as the tracers.

There were holes in the cliff wall they were shooting at, but there was no way in hell anyone was inside them. For one, it was a cliff wall. The Taliban, or whoever, would have either had to scale the wall to crawl into them, or tunnel through the back side of the mountain, which would have taken months even with a whole crew of miners. Second, once they were inside said holes, they'd be totally exposed, prompting them to have to egress back through the mountain once spotted, or plummet two hundred feet to their death. So strategically it made no sense, either. Years later, I'd bring this up with one of their mortarmen. "Who knows, man," he replied. "Those holes could've been there from back during their time with the Russians." This was also highly unreasonable. For it to be true, Weapons Company would have had to have set up their PB in the exact same position across from the cliffs as whatever Russian unit was there before us, and the odds of that were in no way likely.

All of this begged the question: Why were we shooting into a cliff? The answer, I would argue, is twofold: One, the Taliban had taken on mythical status to us, an infinite and indefatigable enemy that struck out from hidden parts of our imagination, like those sand creatures in *Star Wars*, the Tusken Raiders, George Lucas's gift to Western audiences' idea of the Middle East. Dirty, robed, grotesque. Moving from cave to cave invisible to the human eye. Two, the more obvious factor, was that whenever one person started shooting at something it gave the impression to others that he knew what he was doing, and the rest would follow suit. Oftentimes in firefights the goal was simply to make as much noise as possible in the hopes that the enemy would be overcome with sound, if not bullets. Air support was even more capable of administering sonic fear. But unfortunately for us that morning, air support wasn't biting to our requests, and the enemy wasn't even close to the area where we were unleashing our pent-up aggression.

A few guys had spent the previous night down by the river near the cliff fucking around in one of their trucks, and now they were trapped out in the open as 30mm grenade rounds rained from the sky all around them. Puffs of smoke rose as they impacted the ground near the lone truck, the delayed *crunch* coming after, as if a giant were walking across the land. They must have been even more confused than us as we sprayed the .50-cal over their heads into the cliff behind them, and over the radio came a crackled and incoherent barrage of questions, eventually leading to them slowly turning back toward the patrol base.

Everything died down for a while once they got safely back in the wire. Guys were replenishing their rounds and dumping heavy loads of adrenaline, their giddiness spilling out into their voices.

"Did you see how close they got? Did you??" the guys in the truck asked, dopamine glinting off their teeth in wide grins, chain-smoking cigarettes as they replayed the best moments so far like it was *Monday Night Football*. Ortega, a lovable idiot from Texas, was packing a can of dip as he smiled at me. "Whoo!" he exhaled. "Mortar morning."

It was different when things picked up again. As a new 30mm round came down on the roof of one of their mud huts, the platoon commander, Lieutenant Gandy, ordered half of the men back inside the compound. There were groans and arguments about who would go, but eventually it worked itself out, and you could tell some were secretly yearning to get back inside, having already fired enough rounds to warrant their Combat Action Ribbons.

"What about Combat Camera, sir?" someone asked.

"You're good, dude," he said, and lifted a pair of binoculars to his face, scanning the cliff wall for any movement. "Ey!" he shouted, putting the binoculars back down. "Get the fucking 'terp! Get a fucking SP loudspeaker! And tell the fucking civilians to go the fuck back inside!"

There were some locals working on a drainage ditch right outside the PB who hadn't seemed to notice all the commotion; they were hunched over tending to their duties as if nothing unusual was happening at all. The interpreter came out and started shouting at them to go inside, and they sort of stood there incredulously, until one of our machine gunners threatened to open up on them if they didn't move.

"Za, motherfuckers! Za!"

"Run, bitches!" they screamed.

I already had enough footage of them shooting to make a complete package—if I wanted to, I could make it look like D-Day with the right editing—but I was still hoping to get a clear shot of an incoming mortar round. Aside from the kill shot, that was pretty damn high on my priority list, a real Bigfoot type of moment. It was pretty rare to catch enemy rounds impacting on camera because, obviously, you never knew where they were going to land. So I stood around the berm outside the compound scanning the area, and whenever the camera landed on any of the grunts they'd smile and wave back at me.

"Don't do that," I said. "You're under attack."

"Sorry, dude."

We waited like fishermen out at sea for the big one to bite, and the fear congealed into a slow drip, waiting without knowing when and where the next one would hit. Hours passed. "Maybe we're looking in the completely wrong spot," one of them pondered out loud.

BOOM!

TATATATATATA!

They were all screaming again, shooting wildly after a grenade exploded in the branches of a tree not fifteen meters away from us. The camera shook as a quiver worked its way up my spine and out into my hands. *Holy shit, holy shit.* Random tunes started to cycle through my head, stored in the backup hard drive of my mind.

"I just called, to say, I *love you* . . . I just called, to say, how much, I *care* . . ."

"FUCK YOU!!" the turret gunner screamed, as he trained his .50-cal on the small village to our east, no longer bothering with the cliffs.

"YOU'RE GONNA RUN OUT OF FUCKING AMMO!" a squad leader screamed. More silence then, as the gravity of the situation started to avail itself to us like a dark flower of death opening its petals, revealing its true nature. "Are y'all fucking stupid?" he asked. The question was left hanging in the air unanswered.

"Janie's got a gun, Janie's got a gun . . ."

The old childlike fear settled into us, as they started "walking them on," a scary turn of phrase that meant they were measuring their shots with a spotter, and that elicited grade school memories of footsteps coming down the hall after you did something bad. Damn, we thought, They must've been trained by the best, because They sure as shit knew how to use whatever They were shooting.

"They got us dialed in!" someone hollered.

No shit.

We are no longer Marines (whatever those were), we are scared, blubbering kids. Townshend is down, bleeding on the ground; Ortega screams; as for me, it feels like a giant hand has ripped open from the earth and slapped me across the face. The camera drops, the world spins, the crowd goes wild, but never as wild as you hope for.

In my dreams they're still there, half-formed video game sprites ready to materialize from the ether. Sometimes I can't see them but I can feel them, a spidery cancer crawling around the perimeter of my soul, waiting to deliver the blow that will finally free me from all the stupid, shitty things I've done. I disassociate in the chaos. I'm standing outside myself. It's as if we're not really in Afghanistan but in an arena that *resembles* Afghanistan. Muzzle flashes, those things from the movies that we constantly searched for to give a face to our fears, are real for the first time ever, and different places I've been merge together in atemporal fashion. A frozen crowd of people look on distracted as the guy next to me screams muted, "Fucking shoot!" And we jerk it out, the elephant still sitting there on my chest, but it's easier because there finally seems to be a direction that things are going. I'm either going to die, or we'll win; it's as simple as that.

Other guys undoubtedly have it rougher. I'm a basic voyeur here, but when you're in charge of someone and their life is in your hands that's a very different thing. When I asked a platoon sergeant on the medevac ride out if that had been the most accurate IDF (indirect fire) hit he'd ever taken, he looked out of the window of the truck and spat out, "Yes," with such decisiveness that I could tell he was thinking hard about his guys who were hurt. There were five casualties in all: me, Townshend, Jones, who got his nose ripped off, another guy who took a little shrapnel in the leg, and Ortega, though Ortega's injury wasn't visible. When the 30mm grenade hurtled past us I felt a curious heat brush the air, and I thought, *Holy shit, sniper* . . . but it couldn't have been a sniper because bullets either whizz or crack, and that bullet did neither. And as I ran for cover the ground erupted and pushed everything apart. Later they would tell us that the Taliban had these delayed-impact rounds that would land and not go off for a few seconds, giving the impression that it was a dud. Then, once a crowd of soldiers had gathered around to inspect, the round would go off, thereby inflicting the most casualties. Right on cue, we had continued to knee-jerk around, lost in the dance, until it went off and blasted Townshend with shrapnel from his knees up to his face, screaming out, more in fear of what would be there when he got a chance to look than actual pain.

This wasn't Ortega's first concussion. High school football coupled with one too many IED blasts made sure of that. After he grabbed Townshend and dragged him to safety, and the medevac bird came to get him and Jones, he sat down exhausted in the Combat Operations Center and began speaking gibberish. It felt remarkably routine, and everyone laughed it off at first. "Too much excitement in one day for ol' Ortega."

But soon he was drooling and writhing around on the floor, and the doc had to call another medevac to get him out of there. He would end up in the traumatic brain injury ward of the hospital on Camp Leatherneck for a few weeks, where the nurses would come get him every time the video I shot of the attack, which ended up on CNN, came on their TVs. (In the video, I coached Lieutenant Gandy to explain that there were indeed enemy combatants inside the cliff wall, because I needed to make it clean, just as much for myself as for everyone else.)

Ortega got placed on light duty once he was finally discharged from the hospital. The doctors told him that the next blast he took would leave him permanently fried—and he was assigned to basic desk work back on the FOB. I would run into him occasionally in transit and he'd always get real excited. "Hey, man, I saw your video in the hospital! Fuckin' badass, dude!"

"Yeah, man! You're a star," I'd say. But then I'd see him a few weeks later and he'd repeat the same thing, and even a few hours after just having talked to him he'd come up to me and say it again. "Yooo, I saw your video in the hospital, man! Fuckin' badass!" But now there was a twinge of uncertainty in his voice, as if he'd not only seen the video, but had seen this whole movie before. I'd laugh and pat him on the back, but inside I was crying.

I was in good with the Afghan translators on the FOB, and after I got the tiny piece of shrapnel plucked out of my head by the docs ("Purple Heart?" they asked the head surgeon. "Egh," he replied. "We'll give him a freebie"), I went to their tent and ate some of the rice they'd prepared that night. Wahid was one of the saltiest translators we had. He'd been on nine consecutive deployments, with a whole host of different units ranging from Blackwater to special ops, and he wouldn't stop flicking me in the head where my bandage was, talking about how many times he'd been shot.

"Americans are fucking pussies, man," he said. "I've been shot twice on two different deployments. Where is my Purple Heart?" He shook his head at me as if I was a disgrace.

I just brushed him off as a crazy Afghan who'd grown numb to it all, but a part of me wondered if maybe what we Americans referred to so readily as "trauma" wasn't different from what they called it in other places. When we came back from the deployment, for instance, they put me in the hospital. It was an ultimatum; I'd gotten written up (NJP'd) three times in the first two months of our return for drinking-related incidents: one DUI, one fight during the White House Correspondents' Association banquet (which I'd been invited to because of the CNN video), and one time for sneaking Loya off of restriction to go to a strip club. We didn't even have a good time: Loya took a high-heeled Spartan kick to the chest after making an off-color remark to one of the dancers, followed swiftly by an escort to the door by the club's bouncer. I'd never seen anything like it, but when I asked what he'd said to make her react in such a way, Loya wouldn't tell me.

"I have no idea," he said. "I blacked out."

"Damn. Well, maybe one day you'll remember. It'll all come back to you in a drunken flashback."

"I hope so," he said. "It sucks not being able to remember, like, if I wanted to go back and apologize or something. You know I don't say shit to women. I'm not like that." I could hear him almost getting choked up about it, so I didn't bring it up again.

The military psych ward/rehab facility always stank of malaise. People in their pajamas lounging around everywhere, playing foosball or watching TV. Our group counselor was a former Army medic, a stocky Chicana with sharp, white canines and bright red lipstick. Everyone was in love with her because she had convinced them all that they had PTSD, even the guys who hadn't seen combat and were just there to get a break from the bottle, or were sick of dealing with their commanders. She would go around the circle, asking everyone if they had something they wanted to talk about, gently correcting them when their misdirected frustrations found a faulty target.

"Well, for starters, my CO drives me fucking insane," someone would say. "I think a lot of my anger and drinking comes from having to deal with his bullshit all the time."

"Does *he* drive you insane?" she'd ask. "Or is that *your* response to *his* behavior?" Then she'd give a warm chuckle after the guy had amended himself.

"It's not about me, I keep forgetting to tell myself," he'd say.

The ward was thick with the usual slut-shaming gossip that

military guys shared in response to any kind of female attention ("I heard she fucked a guy who was here before you got here," they'd tell me), as brainwashed as we all had been since those first days back in basic training. Sometimes the counselor would come up behind you while you were in one of the common areas and start massaging your shoulders, whisper stuff like, "How you doing? Had any time to think about what we discussed?" and it would drive you nuts with ideas as it blended in with this toxic stew of isolation and testosterone.

The only guy in the hospital who disliked her was my roommate, a nineteen-year-old fresh from some pit stain in Alabama, a real inbred type who was always playing around during our meetings. He'd gotten sent there because he kept getting caught with Spice, the artificial marijuana substitute that they were selling legally in smoke shops and convenience stores everywhere down south. It was big in the military back then because it didn't show up in your urine, so how this kid was getting caught with it was a mystery.

You could tell the counselor wasn't feeling him at all, and she would usually skip over him during our meetings unless he insisted on saying something. We were all pretty much on the same program by the time he showed up. We had taken the instructions she'd given us, the tools, if you will, and were applying them to just about every aspect of our lives. She was impressed with our progress. The kid, however, was less easy to wrangle, and I have to admit, I admired his resilience at first.

"I dunno," he began one day. "I like drinkin' and smokin'. It makes life more interestin', 'specially the fuckin' Army. I mean, shit, what else are you supposed to do in the Army?" He had a face like one of those medieval paintings, slack and aching for detail, from back before they knew how to draw faces yet.

"Sean," she said, "do you ever experience visual impairments after smoking Spice?"

"Whattaya mean?"

"Well, we've been getting lots of people that have trouble tracking movement after prolonged usage."

"Ohhh, you mean like when everything slows down, like in clips, like a photo album or somethin'?"

She nodded.

"Oh, hell yeah, that's the best part!" he exclaimed.

"Well, Sean, how do you think it makes your fellow soldiers feel that your high is more important to you than their safety?"

"Huh?"

"What I mean is that if your vision becomes permanently impaired because of your Spice use, how do you expect to be able to adequately defend them in combat?"

"Man, you're always bringin' that up. I know I haven't deployed yet, but that ain't my fault. You don't think I want to?"

"Well, Sean, there are men here sitting beside you who have deployed and do have real trauma, and for you to sit here and waste their time—"

"How am I wastin' their time?"

"Because you're not taking this seriously."

"Well, fine. Whattaya want me to say?"

"I think we'd all like to know why it is that you have to use substances, the real reasons, not the excuses you make to yourself."

He laughed again. "I told ya already, it genuinely makes life more interestin'."

"Last week we started talking about your mom and dad. . . ."

"Stepdad," he corrected her, looking down at the floor.

"Well, do you want to go deeper into that today?"

He continued looking down at his feet, shuffling them around on the linoleum floor in his hospital-issued Crocs. That's another thing I disliked about the place; everyone's feet were always exposed because they didn't let you wear anything with laces.

"I *hate* that motherfucker," he said eventually.

"Why?"

"Why do you think? He made her do stuff."

"What stuff?"

"God*damn*," he hissed. He was flustered now; you could tell she was wearing him down like she'd worn down the rest of us. But with us it was invited; most of us had secretly come there to be diagnosed. This seemed to be edging toward something perverse.

"Sean," she said. "What did he make her do?"

"Nothin', forget it," he said.

"You're clearly upset."

"Yeah, I'm upset. You would be, too."

"Why, Sean?" She kept going at him while the rest of us silently rubbernecked along with her, until eventually he let it out.

"He made 'er fuck the dog! Is that what you wanna hear?" he shouted, dropping his head in humiliation.

"What?"

"He made 'er fuck our dog and he took pictures! Okay?" Everyone was quiet. "He'd take pictures of her and then he'd post 'em online, the *son of a bitch*!"

Even she wasn't expecting that. She took a beat to hide the discomfort that had translated to her face, a moment of awkwardness while she tried to figure out where to go with it next. "That's . . . that's terrible, Sean. I'm sorry that he did that."

We all thanked him for sharing but there were sly looks going around the circle for the rest of the session. He didn't talk too much more after that. He stopped making wisecracks during the meetings and would listen more intently, but you could tell the revelation didn't sit well, especially how she'd gotten it out of him. I felt bad, and tried not to laugh when the other guys made jokes about it behind his back.

But there were people who had it worse. That's what you always had to tell yourself, that there was a hierarchy for this shit. The whole thing was a trauma-pissing contest for trauma porn addicts.

By far the worst one in there was a captain who had two Purple Hearts and a Silver Star. He was awaiting trial for vehicular manslaughter after he killed a whole family while driving drunk. It happened the night after he came back from his fourth and final deployment, and he had just been awarded for running somewhere under fire or doing some other kind of heroic thing. He never came to any of the group meetings and had his food left outside his room. The few times you'd see him was when he came out to use the phone to talk to his lawyer. Like a ghost of a man, reduced now to a cautionary tale, he would shuffle past us with eyes cast downward, eyes that had no life left in them, no fucks left to give.

His attorney pushed hard for a judge who would grant him leniency, take into account that his drinking stemmed from all the combat he'd seen and that he had been a good Marine who should have gotten the help he needed, etc. For the rest of us in the hospital, PTSD was our ticket to relevance, a badge of honor in many regards, a way to give meaning to the meaninglessness we had endured and to excuse our shitty behavior. I don't mean to say that we went to war in search of a PTSD diagnosis, but just as there's something to the idea that the uniform creates the soldier, cloaking them in a mask of courage that wouldn't be there otherwise, the masks of trauma worn by veterans who return from war allow them to evade critical thought about what they took part in as an instrument of the state. The trauma is a way to meet people's expectations, a bona fide, a lingua franca, or, shit, even to get laid sometimes. It served its purpose, and for the captain, it was a way to avoid a life sentence.

———

Alone time with the counselor usually came toward the end of each soldier's stay. She would take you into her office, a small wedge of a room tucked into one of the corridors of the hospital outside the locked-off area, and get you to "open up." A lot was riding on my meeting with her, because my command was trying to kick me out without benefits. Her write-up would go a long way in showing them that I was capable of being a good Marine. I was confident I could make it through the remaining six months left on my contract without another incident, but still it felt as if the walls were starting to close in. Coming back from deployment where everything was such high stakes exposed the garrison version of military life for what it really was: a farce. The Corps was now trying to cut its numbers after Obama's troop surge and things were supposed to be "winding down" in Afghanistan, so they were looking for things to kick people out for. They would write you up for not shaving or for wearing white socks, instead of the standard-issue green or brown. They would go through our rooms while we were at work and if you hadn't taken your trash out, they'd flip it over and throw garbage everywhere. It seemed like there were traps laid out all over the place. That's when the anger started to flow as freely as the drugs and beer.

My friend Vasquez and I had learned about a spot to buy coke in a trailer park just off base. Word came from an old lady who worked at the chow hall. She approached us one morning while we were hungover, telling us "it seems like you two go pretty hard" as we wolfed down crappy breakfast burritos. Vaz laughed innocently and said we sure did, but I could tell she wasn't just making small talk. I asked her what was up, and she gave us her number and told us to come by anytime.

So, we were driving out there on the freeway and, as always, Vaz was giving me a hard time about money. He never wanted to throw down, and when he did it was always less than what *you* were throwing down because he wasn't going to do as much, or because he had discovered the hookup, or you owed him gas money from another time, or whatever else. I actually didn't mind because he was fun to be around once you finally got the stuff and he stopped whining. But this time he started going on about how we should maybe haggle these trailer park dealers, and see if we could get it for less, because it was coming from a trailer park after all and it probably wasn't the best stuff. That's when I snapped and almost flipped the car doing a U-turn at about sixty into oncoming traffic. We skidded off the road into a ditch with Vaz screaming, and before he could say anything else, I jumped out of the car and pulled him out of the passenger's side. We started tussling on the side of the freeway as other people drove by honking. But when you fought with Vaz it could never just stay on the parameters of the fight. He would get worked up and bring up his family and his life growing up on the streets and how you had no idea, and after a point you just stopped being angry at him because you could see how upset he had gotten.

That's how vets realize they've become more comfortable at war than in the real active chaos of home. In Iraq and Afghanistan death was accepted as a natural state of life—it was in each step you took, each sigh of relief—but in the States it came as a surprise, like you'd been cheated. The pieces didn't fit together anymore. America did its best to make its citizens think death was nonexistent, or that they were already in some state of afterlife. Everywhere you went there were advertisements for things that could make you feel as relaxed and safe as possible, and the more they kept telling you to relax, the crazier it made you feel because maybe they were on to something; maybe you *were* wound a little too tight. You'd be shopping at Walmart and see a sale on stress gummies when the thought would creep into your head: a man livestreaming his mass shooting. And then what? You die in Walmart on GoPro footage that'll get uploaded onto YouTube when you could have died in combat, where Marines were supposed to die. The anger could shield you from these thoughts, because you could tell yourself that, if it were to happen, you would see red and bum-rush the fucker when he wasn't looking. But in reality, the anger was what put you into precarious positions in the first place; the anger was the war's way of saying, "I got you. I got you forever."

I told the counselor I felt comfortable, though, now that I'd been given the right tools and everything. And besides, I was already an angry kid before I enlisted. This was growth. She didn't seem convinced. "I don't think you're ready to leave here, Jake." For some reason, in the hospital, I had decided to give up on correcting them that I'd gone by my middle name, Miles, all my life. On all the forms it was Jacob, but there was also a feeling that I was going to be someone new again, or that maybe my hospital stint would be a separate me, a probationary test run of me, so to speak.

"Really?" I said. I was sort of expecting this. She convinced a lot of guys to stay an extra month or two. But as much as I hated the idea of going back to Camp Lejeune, I was more scared of staying there. I could feel myself getting soft in the hospital, and the place was starting to feel a bit incestuous.

"We haven't gone much into your deployment at all," she said. "You hardly talk during group."

"I've talked a bit," I said with a nervous chuckle. The truth was that this all seemed borderline silly. Sure, I'd seen some stuff, and years later I'd still be getting into bar fights and crying to strangers, but fetishizing trauma and the experience of war in a confined setting just didn't feel genuine. At that moment what I really needed more than anything was to get the hell out of the Marine Corps with an honorable discharge. And she was capable of making that happen.

"I just feel like I don't have PTSD," I confessed.

"Jake, you were hit in the head with shrapnel from a grenade."

"Yeah, but it wasn't that bad. Like, I was actually kind of happy when it happened because I was recording."

"What?"

"I was filming when it happened so I got some really good footage out of it."

She asked me about the other videos I had on my hard drive, videos of ghosts, like the children in the bazaar, or the dead civilian we killed accidentally though maybe on purpose, or a fellow Marine getting shot in the head—a video that, when I showed it to people, made them forget that they weren't watching a Hollywood movie.

"It's like *Black Hawk Down*," they'd say. "It's like Vietnam." Vietnam was no longer synonymous with the war, but with movies of the war. We really don't know how to express anything anymore, other than through movie or TV references, but war is probably the singular thing in American society that can *only* be accessed via movies. It made me proud when they said those things, I have to admit, because that was the goal, that was my holy grail. Saying my crappy handheld videos looked like a movie was akin to saying I had the biggest dick on the planet. It validated everything I'd worked toward while diminishing it at the same time. It made my cinematic dreams come to life, and it made all the suffering less significant. It bridged the realities of life with the surface-level existence of on-screen emotion, which, for the VHS babies, was already a strong bond—for the smartphone babies, it was one and the same.

Did you kill anyone? I couldn't imagine.

You didn't have to imagine anymore. I could show you on my laptop the things you tried to piece together in the digital library of your mind. Ignore the slight contradictions and idiosyncrasies of real death, the sounds a body makes while bleeding out, how soldiers get tired and bicker while carrying their wounded (I'll edit that part out), and enjoy an unadulterated link to the Hollywood War Show. Shit, that's what I made it for. That's what kept me going all those years.

After a while, though, you wonder if you missed something while holding the camera. Did you subconsciously bleep certain things out? I told the counselor I was starting to lose the glue.

"What do you mean?" she asked.

"Like, I don't know if I'm remembering actual memories of what happened, or if I'm just remembering me watching them on my computer." Which I'd done about a hundred times since getting back.

"We need to access those raw memories, then," she said. The metadata, the raw material, the nonfungible token of memory.

I didn't think it was possible. Something interesting happened to me in the last few months of the deployment. I realized I had the capacity not only to lose memories with the camera, but also to create them.

CHAPTER 9

"Nuther Day, Man . . . Nuther Day"

It happened right after one of our designated marksmen got shot in the head and a combat engineer got his legs blown off and we all saw *Avatar* for the first time. Someone got a bootleg version of it on their hard drive and we all gathered to watch it in a mud hut. We were crowded around watching those blue fuckers fly through the air, and I knew with every fiber of my being that this was the beginning of the end for many things that defined us as a society.

We lost three people because they sent an undermanned, over-ambitious, single platoon (that's roughly twenty-five guys) across the Helmand River to set up an outpost in the middle of nowhere. It appeared that the battalion commander, Colonel Rockwell, was thinking we hadn't really done enough war for the past six months of the deployment, and his chest was feeling a bit empty in terms of the ribbons he was hoping to come back with. Any time the BC orchestrated a little troop movement, he received a Bronze Star with combat *V* for valor. It made sense, if you think about it, because it takes balls to accept an award for sending other people to do something suicidal.

One could say I had been willingly roped into this mission. There was only a month left on our deployment before we were set to go home, and the platoon they chose had been selected because they hadn't been doing much for the past six months beyond keeping watch on a few detainees back at the FOB. They woke up each morning, stood watch around the airstrip, and made sure nobody tried to scale the jagged hills overlooking the base to take an RPG shot at one of the incoming aircraft.

They had also informally picked up the job of Afghan Army social coordinator. They would hold lots of shuras and meetings with them and the locals, engagements that would usually end with everyone feeling more confused about what we were supposed to be doing than they were before the meeting began.

The platoon had been hearing bombs drop across the river all week; a MARSOC team was sent out there—those burly guys who acted holier than thou because they were allowed to grow beards and didn't have to wear uniforms—and within the first two days of them getting there, they lost one guy and took another casualty— a double amputee—then quickly retreated back to Camp Leatherneck. They needed some fresh souls to take over the area, and we were next up.

The Afghan campaign was full of these overly simplistic missions, whereby someone would get it in their heads that we were done sitting around waiting to get blown up, and needed to go out and take the fight to the enemy instead. It was real cowboy shit, and the Marines loved it because it felt like we were in an actual war; we'd get to ride in a helicopter and maybe see the enemy at some point. People didn't get as turned on when you told them you lived in someone's mud hut for seven months, and each morning would get up and walk a one-mile perimeter around it, talking to random locals in the area and waiting for an invisible foe to take a shot at you or blow your legs off. They wanted to hear about night raids and ambushes, close-quarters combat where you could see the whites of the enemy's eyes, and how it felt to kill a man.

I first met Lance Corporal Platt when they were gearing up for the helo insert. He had seen the CNN video I made and was already envisioning himself as the U.S. military's next TV star. He was about as Marine a Marine as you could find. He was planning to stay in the Corps for life, go to Sniper School, work his way up the ladder to first sergeant, and then, eventually, maybe even become the next sergeant major of the Marine Corps. I knew he was dangerous because he seemed to love being in Afghanistan. The ones who you had to watch out for were not the druggies or shitbags, but the guys who actually believed in what we were doing, because they were all set to really go the extra mile. There were things that, if you were a rational person, you accepted as impossible in Afghanistan. For instance, you could not go chasing the Taliban. They had egress routes out the wazoo and were able to easily blend into the civilian population. Chasing them could only lead to getting stuck somewhere you shouldn't be, which was usually their intention in the first place. Platt was a Taliban chaser. There was no nuance to his view of the war; in his eyes we were doing the Lord's work by "killing hajis," giving them a "dose o' freedom," as he'd say. He believed that he was defending America by fighting the Taliban, straight up.

He even asked if I wanted to get a pre-op interview before the mission started, a first for me as a cameraman.

"I'm not telling you how to do your job, bro, I'm just sayin' it would be pretty sick if people could see the before and after," he said.

How could I be upset? The guy was a Combat Cameraman's

wet dream. To him, I wasn't just an afterthought like I was with most platoons (someone they'd have to make space for and look after); I was mission critical. He had pretty much single-handedly convinced their platoon leader, Lieutenant Anderson, a milky bro type from Wisconsin who was a little soft at heart, to let me come along and film them. He sat him down and showed him the CNN video, with the grenade hit and Townshend, the one who was hit the worst, getting dragged (which I muted and put in slow motion to add drama), and then Ortega carrying a bloody pile of bandages while saying to the camera, "Nuther day, man . . . nuther day" (before he blacked out from traumatic brain injury) and Lieutenant Anderson stood up firmly and pointed at me and said, "You're coming with us."

"You got enough batteries? You got enough tapes?" Platt asked me as we were getting ready. "Ain't gonna be no electricity out there so you gotta bring everything you can. Shit's gonna pop off so you're gonna wanna bring backups of everything too." Then he smiled at me like a fucking hero. Tennessee sunshine in his eyes.

I loved Platt, like I would come to love all of them, even after everything went wrong and they all turned on him. Marines can be drama queens. They want to blow stuff up and shoot their guns and "get some," but they don't want to see each other die. It didn't make sense to me; or perhaps it did make sense, but it still felt naïve. Because you couldn't have one without the other. The stakes of war were such that you and the people you knew might have to die. That was the catch. You couldn't say you'd seen some shit if no one from your unit had gotten maimed or killed. It was the dirty secret of the infantry; each unit summed each other's deployment up by how many KIAs they'd taken, how many Purple Hearts or "Taliban Marksmanship" badges they had. And they knew this. But when the reality came in and they lost their friends, they wanted to act like there had been some kind of mistake.

Sergeant Lopez, the platoon sergeant of Second Platoon, was making everyone laugh on the airstrip at 3 a.m., which attested to his oratorical skills, because this was a very dangerous and stupid mission, and we were all getting cold feet, feeling a bit like maybe it would be best to just postpone the whole thing and crawl back into bed. He was telling a story about falling into a wadi, a story that everyone had a version of because everyone had fallen into a wadi at some point or another. But he was making us laugh because of the way he described it, with his body cartoonishly frozen in mid-air over the make-believe wadi, head turning back to look at the Taliban, or whoever was trying to shoot him in the ass. The punch line was that it wasn't the Taliban, but another squad of Marines who had mistakenly been shooting at him the whole time. This happened a lot as well.

He got unexpectedly serious and said to the group, "Ain't gonna bullshit you. Some of y'all ain't coming back from this one." He looked at the sky, waiting for the chopper to come in, while the rest of us looked down at our feet stupidly.

I could feel the helicopter approaching and, neurotically, I checked my camera bag for the hundredth time. I loathed helicopters. They were obnoxious and reeked of oil. The pilots who flew them were bad at their jobs and would often crash. I had heard that the number one killer of Marines during training exercises was helicopter crashes. Being inside one was like getting beat up from within your own body, and I always prayed they'd stick the landing slowly, because whenever I flew in one, especially Ospreys, they would always make it to the destination, hover five feet over the ground for an hour, then abruptly hit the deck with a gut-wrenching thud, and you'd feel your ass bone connect with the back of your skull. I hated helicopters.

The thing came down into the airstrip, making as much noise and blowing as much debris around as possible, and we all loaded into it one by one with our rucks strung around the fronts of our bodies so we could sit down as soon as we got to our seats. The door gunner was jumping around deliriously, shouting and waving us on board, and I tried not to look at him because he looked really stupid, and I didn't want to think about him and ruin the serious thoughts I had in my head. I was thinking about fear and the acknowledgment of fear, and I was thinking about what my friends from high school would think if I died. Why did he do it? they'd wonder. So random, they'd say. At least it wouldn't be as bad as our friend Dakota. He shot himself our senior year, after we'd all witnessed his increasingly erratic behavior (randomly kicking in subway car windows with his Timberlands while hanging from the handrails, quoting Travis Bickle from *Taxi Driver* in an unironic way), but we had done nothing about it because we were all competing to see who was king crazy, who was actually bull-goose loony, and we didn't want to seem pussy about it like we were "concerned for him" or anything. Maybe it wouldn't be that different from Dakota if I died. Maybe the only way to become king crazy was to die.

The bird took off, lurching sharply, and we sat in the dark with our night-vision goggles and thought about our lives. I could feel the oil dripping from the ceiling and tasted its rheumatic, phlegmy essence like pharmacy woes in the back of my throat. I pulled out my camera and started filming the beginning of the operation. Each one of them soon to be characters in the greatest war movie of all time. Doc Coleman, the Navy corpsman, the "I got you, baby, doc's here, nobody gets hurt while doc's here" (he actually said stuff like that, I couldn't believe it); Lance Corporal Sabbagh, a skinny Muslim Marine with the voice of a redneck; Corporal Edwards, a combat engineer with the face of a little boy; Derrickson, an awkward infantry assault Marine specializing in demolitions and who the others were sure was a homosexual; some more guys who fit the various character tropes while also subverting them; and, of course, their squad leader, Lance Corporal Platt, who was already flashing a backward peace sign at the camera before I even got to him.

Suddenly I heard a shout, as a fat-gloved hand came down on my camera, almost smashing the lens hood off. I sat there stunned for a second, as I considered ways that I could get out of my seat and lunge at the door gunner, who was shouting something about the light from the camera attracting the enemy, but I was too weighed down by my rucksack to do anything. I wriggled around helplessly.

"WE'RE IN A FUCKING HELICOPTER!" I screamed at him. "YOU DON'T THINK THEY HEAR US COMING?"

I was so angry I could feel tears forming around the edges of my eyes. But he couldn't hear me over the sound of the engine, and he had bounced over to do something else anyway, the stupid rope that kept him from falling out of the helicopter dangling behind him. I seethed at the idea that he thought he'd done some kind of valiant and reasonable act by almost breaking my camera.

We came down and, sure enough, sat hovering for forty minutes, just to make sure the enemy had plenty of time to dial us in, then dropped like a bloated whale onto the dirt. We all shuffled out and formed a little circle around the helicopter and tried not to get hit with any rocks as it took off.

It was quiet for a while, until somebody said calmly in the dark, "So there I was . . . balls deep," in that loose Virginia twang that made everything sound sexual. We all giggled. I looked over and saw that it was Sergeant Elmira, a pink-faced ginger who looked even more like a White supremacist with the wispy, blond mustache he kept dangling over his lip. He and Lopez had had some disputes over who would be platoon sergeant, and I think there was some racial components to that discussion that resulted in Elmira being dropped from platoon sergeant to squad leader. Racial squabbles in the Marines usually ended either in fists or with someone more senior (usually an officer) getting involved.

We got up eventually and walked over to a compound on the hill ahead of us. We paid off the family who lived there and told them to leave (hearts and minds 👍), and as the sun came up, we all saw the strange, hilly landscape unveiled before us, with biblical labyrinthine complexes of mud huts and strange, archaeological fixtures in the rocks that looked like enemy fighting holes (or maybe not; we were programmed to see everything that way). The pattern of things seemed layered with meaning, if you could just look at it for long enough and feel the weight of the place without instinctively scanning for "murder holes," "military-aged males," or "spotters."

There was no green in this area, just moon-rock desert, and the people were bone thin. The ones in the houses closest to us came outside, looked up warily to our new spot on the hill, and, realizing their vicinity to us, scratched their heads and pondered whether to pack up and leave, because they were surely going to get caught in the crossfire. Directly to our south was the Helmand River, which was not so much a river in this area as it was a man-made irrigation system that flowed from the Kajaki Dam. It was the main source of water for all the poppy fields in the area, and some of the guys were already talking conspiracy theories about how we were actually securing the dam on behalf of the pharmaceutical industry so they could keep the poppy business going and get us hooked on opioids when we got back to the States all fucked up and traumatized. Is it still ironic if the irony was always expected?

We regrouped and ate our shitty MRE breakfasts—chicken with dumplings (chicken with a question mark because it tasted like tuna fish), spaghetti, and other pastas that said on the back of the packages they were made in a factory in Brooklyn—and we waited for the fun to start. But nothing happened for the first couple of days, as the Taliban let us get comfortable, observing our daily routine. Platt would lead us out in the morning, making sure that I came every time to get shots of him posing and talking with the locals. He pulled me aside during our second patrol and showed me a coloring book he'd taken from a kid with what looked like stick-figure airplanes drawn in it.

"Yup. Ya see right here," he said, holding it up to the camera. "They got the kids drawin' pictures of 9/11, brainwashin' 'em."

I fought the urge to tell him they were actually just drawing us, owners of the things they saw flying over them all the time. I looked up at the sky and tried to imagine a helicopter with no context of what a helicopter was. The people in these areas were un-identified, undocumented by the laws of the twenty-first century; they had unwittingly evaded the reach of the global technological system. We had to retinal-scan them and fingerprint them with our BAT systems (Biometric Analysis Tracking) just so that we could get them onto our radar, keep them organized in some way, because if not they were just out there existing, and we couldn't have that. We had surveillance drones and spy blimps in the skies with state-of-the-art cameras that would monitor them day and night, waiting anxiously for one of them to walk outside and start digging a hole so that we could blow them away. Mostly, though, the lance corporals chugging Rip Its all night in the Combat Operations Center would be looking for late-night goatfuckers, an enduring theme of Operation Enduring Freedom.

We had all this incredibly complex, invasive equipment and we were still losing the war. The same drones we used in Afghanistan would be utilized without people's knowledge a few years later during the Freddie Gray protests in Baltimore, and it was always eerie to see desert-camouflaged military accessories (they didn't even bother getting new paint jobs) being adopted by the cops in New York. It made you wonder: Was it all just an endless experiment for us to try out our new toys, technology that would inevitably be recycled back onto American soil? I would get paranoid thinking the war was following me, as I'd stop and stare at an MRAP sitting in the middle of the projects in Harlem.

The porousness of our wars, which were seeping interchangeably into our homeland, seemed to be part and parcel of the steady slip in other areas. The increased dependency on conspiracy theories and other fairy tales to give us a false sense of agency, the ease with which technology had become our number one addiction, more than a part of our lives but the thing controlling everything. Police brutality.

I linked it all back to *Avatar* at the end of the day. If you could blur the lines of reality that well, what else could you blur? These were real concerns.

We took our first contact the third day while Ali, our interpreter whose name was not actually Ali (we never bothered to find out his real name), was on patrol with us listening to enemy Icom radio traffic. Suddenly he stopped and said, "They want to shoot . . ." and everyone looked at him and said, "Who?" and he said, "Talib," and we all glanced around with a funny clairvoyance, as we felt the crosshairs of the enemy upon us. Some ran for cover, not waiting for the death clap of shots to ring out, while others continued to bask in the enemy's murderous gaze. It was weird, getting an actual trigger warning like that, and you could see why the Taliban put a higher price on the heads of Afghans like Ali, because having them on our side was basically cheating.

I was in a little rivulet in the ground with another guy's boots in my face as I tried to get my camera out of my pouch and start recording. The sky flew around the viewfinder as I felt myself enter its frame, and for a second it felt like I could transport anywhere, that the haptic flare of the lens and the sun would one day reveal to us how we can leave our own bodies while watching homemade combat videos on the internet. Did we find comfort in the real, or was there a new real replacing the old one?

The *clap*s came from enemy AK-47s, followed by the *dub-dub-dub* of the reverb as the bullets went bouncing out through the valley, and I felt the jolt in my chest that always brought me back to the now.

"Everybody wave to the Taliban," someone said. And they opened up on random targets that were not real targets at all: "the green door over there," "the fuckin' mound of dirt over here." We ran giddy through the AO calling in air support every chance we got, trying to collect as much wartime-destruction experience as we could. Hellfire and JDAMs; this is me, represent.

"I'm Bam Margera, and this is winning hearts and minds," one of them said as he held his finger down on the trigger of his 240 until the thing was about to go flying out of his hands. "Mi vida, mi lucha," it said on his sleeve tattoo. I almost couldn't keep up. They wanted everything on camera, even when they ran into each other like idiots or tripped over themselves from adrenaline overload.

"Hey, YouTube, did you get that?" asked a rifleman with blood dripping from his nose after falling and ramming it into the butt-stock of his own weapon.

"I got it." And I'd add it to the moto reel of the day, playing with the saturation and color of the footage to make the blood pop even more. I even toyed with adding fake muzzle-flash effects so that people could get an idea of where we were getting shot at from, even though 95 percent of the time we didn't have a clue.

This was war in the twenty-first century, sprinkled with millennial lust; it was a game we'd been playing since we were kids throwing water balloons at cars, breaking people's hood ornaments, and killing prostitutes in *Grand Theft Auto* late at night while our parents were asleep. It was hide-and-go-seek with higher stakes. They shoot three rounds at us, we drop a two-hundred-pound bomb on the wrong house, then look at each other like, "Oh, shit."

Reach out and touch someone.

We were the first kids to start moving to the rhythm of internet Vines, cutting our laughter and callousness at the moment just before we had context for what we were doing. I filmed a desert crab crawling through a dried-up wadi, then slowly panned up to a Marine looking down at it while licking his chops. "Mmm," he said. "Shit crab." I filmed a goat strapped to a guy's motorbike as he came barreling down the road at us, then hit a bump and almost snapped the goat's neck, its mouth frothing as it brayed out in pain, me zooming in slowly, adding a flare of faux drama, then pulling out to a group of Marines laughing hysterically. Absurdity and contradictions were the cornerstones of war. It was what our DIs in boot camp embodied with their insane behavior, and that led us down a dark corridor of comfortability to the otherness of our occupation, and the letdown of combat. Mostly our DIs had given us the gift of laughter; the ability to find the suffering of other people absolutely tickling.

And the camera fueled all of it.

Soon enough, though, the Old Fear was back, which was good given the general air of invincibility some of us were displaying. Sergeant Elmira was drawing dicks on a few mortar rounds he was hoping to drop on the enemy at some point, and some guys were over by the river trying to figure out a way to get across it so we didn't have to keep flying helos out to drop off food and water to our position. The second night we were there, a Chinook helicopter came soaring in low with a giant crate of MREs hanging off it. We were providing security under some power lines, which the pilot didn't see, and he came in and clipped the cords with the crate, showering us with sparks of electricity. The Chinook got spooked by this, probably thinking they were getting shot at, and promptly flew off, taking the food with them. So, instead we had to pay off a kid and his dad to use an old, overturned top half of a car as a boat to ferry us back and forth across the river. We all joked that it was like *Saving Private Ryan* whenever we got on board the thing—the first beach landing in Afghanistan's history—but then the Taliban started shooting rocket-propelled grenades and recoilless rifles at us while we were out there floating around. They'd arch their rockets into the sky from almost a klick away on the off chance that it might land somewhere near us, and the first time they tried it, it actually did. There were a handful of guys in the "boat" when the first rocket came down in a field not too far off. The thing started seesawing as the guys in it crouched down in surprise, the weight of their gear and strain of their movement almost capsizing it. The kid holding the rope used to keep the thing in line ran for cover, leaving the Marines in the boat stranded.

The Taliban fired off another RPG and everyone in the compound tried to see if the trail of smoke would lead us back to where it came from. The rocket landed somewhat close to the river again, and a guy on post at the corner of the roof looked back and asked, "Are those guys still out on the boat?"

The boat was rocking back and forth and the guys on it were laughing and shitting themselves simultaneously. One of them, Boone, a wooly mammoth of a man, jumped into the river and almost sank to the bottom, but resurfaced quickly and said it wasn't that deep. Slowly, he made his way across.

"Where the fuck is that kid?" he growled, getting out sopping wet and panting. He grabbed the rope and steadied the boat, and the others started pulling themselves across.

Elmira was glad to get the opportunity to use those dick rounds he had drawn up and began dropping them into the mortar tube. *DOOF!* They went off, flying sky-high, reaching the pinnacle of American exceptionalism, then down, marking the world with Elmira's art.

Platt came running over and grabbed me. "C'mon, YouTube, we're goin' out!" he said.

"Wait a minute," Elmira said. "Where the fuck y'all goin'?"

"I saw where they're shootin' 'em from! It ain't that far out!" Platt hollered.

"Well, you still gotta wait till we call it in, motherfucker. Hold on." Elmira went over to the radio, cursing Platt under his breath. "Motherfucker's too gung ho." Elmira was in Iraq three or four times so he was pretty nonplussed with what he referred to as Platt's "motardedness." Platt had been pushing Elmira to get him on a promotion board so he could pick up corporal and finally become a noncommissioned officer, but Elmira told me he didn't think Platt was ready for it. Platt didn't think enough about his guys when he made decisions, just himself, his own personal ambitions, his own private glory.

Elmira and the lieutenant called us out on the radio, "Five packs leaving the wire," and we went through the back door, where we were met with the *crack* of an AK-47 that was so loud it pushed Platt and Sabbagh back against the wall cursing, and we all went back in the house and came out through the front door instead. I started doing this thing I'd been doing since I got hit with the grenade where I'd exhale sharply through my nostrils repeatedly, over and over, like a dumb horse. It often fucked up a lot of my shots, because you can hear me doing it behind the camera. Soon they'll have tiny VR drones flying around our wars, and you won't have to worry about these kinds of things anymore. In the future, you'll be able to zoom out to get a bird's-eye view of things, like after you die in online shooter games, and go floating through the map to see the other players fighting it out, moving up and out, through walls and bodies, the never-ending of atomic digital.

"We gotta run to that berm over there!" Platt cried. I looked over and saw a little mound of dirt in the middle of a field.

"That's not big enou—" I started saying, but he was already off. We all sprinted behind him, our flaks and dump pouches and ammo clattering around like clunky robot appendages, so weighed down by our own gear that, from a distance, we probably looked like turtles shuffling baby-step through the sand ("you see a Marine lying on his back in the middle of the desert"), and when we finally got to the berm, we all collapsed down against it. Some more shots split the air nearby, but this time it sounded like they were coming from behind us. We sat there for a while, feeling stupid and exposed. Platt got on the radio to ask for guidance on where the shots were coming from. No response.

"Hey, Platt," I said, putting on a slight southern accent as I always did with him, "maybe we should get out of here and move to better cover, or something." Platt scanned the area disappointedly. A farmer came driving through the field in a tractor, giving us a wave.

Sabbagh agreed. "Yeah, man, we're pretty exposed here." He jutted his neck out, tensing and untensing it, a tic he seemed to have developed since we'd gotten across the river.

Platt glanced over at me with one eye still glued to the scope of his rifle. "Ey, man, why aren't you recording this?"

———

The loudest claps I ever heard came down on us, followed by the unmistakable heart attack of a *whiz,* like razor-wire contrails splicing the distance between your ears and your heartbeat. Platt screamed "Oh, shit!" jumped up, and started beelining it for a mud hut a few hundred feet away. More breathing and clanking, trying to steady the spinning of the world into a tunnel vision so that we could get where we needed to be safe. When we all got inside, I lit a cigarette and smoked the whole thing down in about three pulls.

"Tell me you got that, YouTube!" Platt said. I shook my head. He pulled his rucksack off and showed me where a bullet had gone through it, pierced his happy suit (a sleeping bag/onesie we wore in cold weather), and gone out the other side. "Whoo! That's a close one," he exhaled triumphantly.

"Of course you get shot through your pack, Platt," Sabbagh said, laughing while still jutting his neck out. Another guy from their company had gotten hit in the Kevlar, he told me. "Platt had to try an' one-up him."

Doc Coleman had mentioned privately to me how he thought Platt was beginning to look a lot like this other kid from their platoon who'd gotten sent home at the beginning of the op and was awaiting court-martial. Murphy was his name, and his was a scandal of legendary proportions. When we'd first arrived in country, Murphy was disheartened because our deployment didn't live up to his D-Day dreams, and we weren't hanging off helicopters or napalming villages. He began to feel an urgency to make something happen.

Nobody had gotten the time to really know him, but my guess was that Murphy had been birthed into an uber-military town somewhere, a place where every swinging dick had a war story, and every coffee shop and bar honored its veterans with the kind of silent adulation that comes from knowing they've seen and done things that should not be discussed.

It's incredible the amount of social currency that comes with being a combat vet in certain places in America, and the way those crusty VFW-hat-wearing relics go shuffling around, clinging desperately to their previous identities, just goes to show: a lot of Americans don't have much to offer. You take away their two, four, ten, or however many years of service, and there's nothing left that defines them.

Murphy was on patrol the first week or so, and he had split off from the rest of his squad to go check out a room in one of the compounds they were hanging out around. That's when the guys heard a blast and came running back to find Murphy staggering out of the compound with his ears ringing, looking around dazed and confused. He wasn't hit with shrapnel but he was clearly concussed, and everything indicated that he had triggered a small but substantial enough IED to warrant a Purple Heart. It made sense—IEDs were often planted in doorways and other places inside compounds. I knew guys who would turn Afghan soldiers into dummy shields, pushing them through doorways first so that they would consume the brunt of the blast. At some point, the command had issued an order stating that the Afghans would have to be the point men on every patrol—part of the illusion that we were transitioning out and the Afghan Army was taking over—but I only ever saw them take the lead when we were stepping through a doorway or other suspected IED areas.

But then it happened again. This time in another compound while Murphy was, again, by himself. Now the whole command was concerned because each squad was equipped with Thor IED jammers, devices that disabled the connection of cell phone–operated IEDs (don't ask me how). If Murphy was getting blasted by all these IEDs, that must have meant something was wrong with the Thors. The DoD began an investigation and was about to recall every one of them from Afghanistan, until they discovered traces of an American grenade and an M203 grenade launcher round in a dirt sample from one of Murphy's blast sites. He had blown himself up with a grenade the first time, then shot a 203 into the corner of the room the second.

"The motherfucker got away with it the first time," Doc said to me. "It's not like you get any special benefits from having *two* Purple Hearts."

"I think he wanted to take shrapnel," Sergeant Elmira said.

I had to look Murphy up on social media when I got out, because I thought they had to be making him up. Sure enough, I found him on Facebook, posts dating back to 2013 when he'd gotten out of the brig; him standing there in his service alphas looking like he hadn't slept in a week, asking in the comments section if anyone had any photos of him with the rest of the guys from the platoon. No one had responded, except for a woman (his aunt maybe) asking, "Are you back in the military?"

Platt was not on Murphy's level, but there was a glancing concern among the other guys that he was trying a little too hard, getting a little too comfortable with the fire burning around us. My animal instinct since arriving in Afghanistan, and seeing how terrifying real combat could be, was to film, to render flat the things that were trying to kill us—put them in a box on my screen so we could all watch to get by. Platt was a character in my movie, and he loved it because the camera helped define him. But he was also crazy. Like Murphy, I think he shared a perverse yearning to get burned, to feel the war on its most intimate level, a glimpse that could only be achieved by tasting the hot sting of shrapnel, feeling the teeth rattle in your head after an IED blast, or, if you really wanted to push it, getting the wind knocked out of your soul from a sucking chest wound. Guns to redneck kids are what skateboards are for city kids. People like Platt had grown up shooting rifles for so long that their power to kill had become less present in their minds. *Go*, the voice in his head said. *Why not go a little more?*

We started going out at night, setting up in a compound, and then waiting till morning when another squad would walk out as bait. Then, when the Taliban started shooting at that bait squad, the troops set up in the compound would try to locate where the fire was coming from. Some strange things happened as a result of this tactic:

A man, not expecting us to be there, climbed over the wall of the compound we were set up in while we were tracking the bait squad. He was almost gunned down by everyone inside, as they turned their rifles on him thinking he was some kind of suicide bomber, but actually he said he was just coming by to collect some things. Ali asked him, if you live in the compound, why are you climbing over the wall? The man said he lost the keys. He quickly showed us that he knew where everything was, pulling out pots and pans and lighting a fire in the hut that served as a kitchen, and offered to make us lunch. We had the best meal of the whole deployment that afternoon (chicken with rice and potatoes), while potshots mingled interchangeably with the crackle of timber from the man's cooking fire, Rosales drawing the Taliban's shots with a Kevlar attached to the end of a stick.

On another night, we shot a dog. It had been left chained to a stake in the ground outside the abandoned house we were taking over and was going rabid. In the morning, when two little girls came to play with it and found it lying in a pool of its own blood, the Taliban started shooting at us and we put the girls in a room where they'd be safe. The shots sounded close, and Platt took me and a couple of other guys through the winding labyrinth of mostly abandoned compounds to go looking for the shooters, keeping his rifle up and at the ready, giving the other guys hand signals while they kind of shuffled incredulously behind him. He kicked in a door, where we found a giant hole in the ground, which Platt examined and said was probably an egress route with a system of tunnels that the Taliban was using. This was why we couldn't ever spot them. To me, it just looked like a giant hole in the ground—I couldn't see any tunnels—but I recorded a shot of it for intel purposes. A day or two later, Lieutenant Anderson asked to see the footage of the tunnel, because Platt kept bringing it up to him, and I got my camera and went scouring through my files to find the clip. For once, my job served a purpose.

But when I looked for it, I couldn't find it anywhere. I thought maybe I'd forgotten to hit record, but there was also a strange, hallucinatory premonition that the hole had never existed in the first place, or that maybe the Taliban had snuck into our base and deleted the clip from my camera.

We were starting to get desperate. We were losing weight from having to run everywhere, and we weren't getting any closer to finding out who exactly had been shooting at us or from where. We almost suffered a heat casualty when one of the new kids, who was lugging the Thor IED jammer around, collapsed during a firefight while we scrambled from one mud hut to another. We saw the look of existential dread come over him, that fishlike, panicked look that people get when they feel their mind slipping away like beaded dots of mercury dancing across a table, and we all felt it, too.

Our luck changed slightly when one of the squads found an old Russian mortar tube chilling in the center of someone's house. An old man came walking by, and they snatched him up and took him back to our patrol base to question him. The next morning, I was making my rounds (to the makeshift toilet we'd created from two stacks of sandbags) when I saw Sergeant Lopez and the LT choking the man and hitting him in the face, while Ali stood anxiously behind them questioning him. The old man looked tired. I paused for a moment, reached for my camera, then stopped and quickly went on my way before they could see me. I could hear the sharp yet muffled sounds of them interrogating the guy, and thought about why I had wanted to film them, and why my first thought wasn't to stop them. Then I thought about why I wasn't doing anything currently to stop them, and by the time I'd finished, sealed my wag bag, and thrown it into our burn pit, I wasn't thinking about it at all.

I woke up at 4 a.m. the next day to the sound of Ali howling at Sergeant Elmira. We were going to set up in another compound, repeating the same routine for the seventh or eighth day, but when Elmira had gone to wake Ali up that day, he wouldn't get out of bed. Elmira went back in and decided to act like a real hard-ass with this man we'd entrusted our safety to while we played empire inside his country.

"Okay, bitch, get up right now. We're leaving in five," he said.

That's when Ali lost it on him. "I am not a Marine!" he screamed. "You don't say bitch to me! I'm tired! My legs are tired! Why do we keep waking up in the middle of the night?" Ali's voice was shrill like a wounded animal's, and it pierced through the already painful night/early morning air. It made those of us within earshot want to crawl away, back to a different time of our lives, a time when maybe we weren't Marines, either.

"I can leave right now if I want to," he said, pointing out to the horizon, where the moonlight played holochrome with the rocks, where a stranger could become even stranger walking across its alien glow. "I can quit whenever I want, and you will have no one to tell you when they're going to shoot."

Elmira got real bashful and apologetic in response. He knew inside that he had gone somewhere he shouldn't have. But Ali wasn't about to let it slide. Afghans can hold a grudge forever, and Ali had clearly run out of patience.

He was wrong about one thing, though: he couldn't walk away, none of us could. Most certainly not me. We were all one of the grunts now, whether we liked it or not.

CHAPTER 10

Observer's Paradox

*I*only really met you once but it seemed like you were good, and the memory *of your goodness distorts everything else that you might have been. I didn't get a chance to know everyone because of my job, moving constantly and only making friends with the loudest and most boisterous people from each platoon because they wanted to be on camera, and they made for the most interesting material. But you were nice. I don't use that term in a perfunctory or superficial way, like when people say, "Oh, he/she is nice," but in the sense that you seemed like you had been raised the old southern way, with manners, and a deep, intense love for your mother, and I remember you asking to sit with me in the chow hall before the shit show that was the river op started, and that you said you were a combat replacement for Murphy, ironically enough. Perhaps you had to be polite, because you were new to the unit, but I remember a noble kind of shine to you, and that you were tough and quieter and more chivalrous than the others, and that you were an ethnic unicorn: a Native American Jew.*

But you also make me wonder about goodness and bravery, and if to be truly brave you have to be dumb, to not really think through the whatabouteries of ethics and fear, to serve only your brothers-in-arms, and to impress upon them that this crazy thing called war wasn't so scary after all. Because the way you died was dumb; there's no two ways about it. All the deaths in Afghanistan were in vain, for sure, but yours didn't need to happen the way that it did.

Platt had started to take us farther and farther outside our AO. We had a limit of where we were supposed to patrol and he was pushing way past it. Lieutenant Anderson could have told him to stop, but that would have required explaining to Platt why he shouldn't be doing his job as hard as he was. One day he led us to the last compound in the maze before the area dropped out into a long, empty space of nothingness, across from which was another cluster of compounds about five hundred meters out. The mud huts at the end of the maze were even more abandoned and slipshod than the others. They were missing pieces and looked as though a giant toddler had clumped them together haphazardly with Play-Doh.

The houses staring at us from across the field had clearly been bombed by the MARSOC guys who were there before us. Everything reeked of slow war and stalemate. These series of mud huts had probably been bombed and abandoned, then bombed and abandoned again, over and over since the start of the war. Platt set us up at the front and each side of the compound so we had security at each point of entrance, and he looked out across the field to where we knew, finally, with near certainty, the bad guys were. We had exhausted every other possibility. If they weren't out there, then they were actual ghosts, and the mysticism and otherness that we attached to Afghanistan was warranted.

We set up in this place that will always be seared in our memories as the death house, and we waited.

It is forever weird and gross and wrong that this death house is available for you to view at your leisure on iTunes, Amazon, or whatever other streaming platform it pops up on next, and that you can see the demise of our friend Lance Corporal Noah Bernhard in painstaking, 4K, high-resolution detail. You can watch Platt order Bernhard onto the roof with Sabbagh, Doc squatting awkwardly in a corner of the compound like a concerned mother telling Bernhard to stay the fuck down, then Bernhard shouting, "Ey, I got one of 'em!" as he popped off rounds on his M14, amazed and in disbelief that he was actually spotting the enemy for the first time in his life, engaging them, finally making contact, before the ripping sound of metal on metal that is a bullet striking his Kevlar and tearing around to the back of his skull, amplified but deadened by the acoustics of the mud walls; the "U of sound," as Loya would say. You can see the discomfort of lifting an unconscious body off a roof without causing them more damage. You can watch as the bandages unravel from Bernhard's blood-soaked head (which some people mistake for brain matter) and hear his moaning voice as the cognitive functions of his rear visual cortex start to wither and collapse. You can see Doc Coleman's large, black arms—the same arms that had assuaged us that no one would get hurt—set him down and try to reset his bandages in vain, cursing, because there is nothing much for a field medic to do about a gunshot wound to the head. And you can hear Sabbagh reassure Bernhard that he's going home and will be all right, he's gonna see his mom soon, even though it is clear Bernhard doesn't even know who or what he is anymore. Bernhard was no longer Bernhard, but that was what they always said when someone got hit. It's what Third Platoon told Townshend when he got hit with that grenade, comforting him by talking about his family, and all the Oxys he was going to get when he got to the hospital; it's what soldiers have been saying to each other since the dawn of morphine. Big momma morphine coming to take you on the last train home, back to the Land of the Big PX, where being carried by your fellow Marines morphs into being carried by your mother through a shopping mall in North Carolina. The weightlessness of the fragrances.

If you're watching you can see them realize that Bernhard still had a stick of MRE gum in his mouth, and watch as they bashfully try to flick it out so he doesn't choke. You can hear Platt complain to Doc, "We gotta get outta here, *bro*," the bro in this case both a plea and a reprimand, and Doc growling back, "I know! His shit came off." And you can see the physical manifestation of dread as Sabbagh's neck twitch starts to get a bit out of control, and he begins jerking his head back and forth violently like a twerked-out chicken, holding Bernhard's limp body in his lap.

"I need you to drag him, Sabbagh. I can't have you afraid to touch him right now, I need you to drag him," Platt was saying.

You can see the futility of air support, which kept coming down to medevac Bernhard but then flying off as soon as we'd get near them, because of small arms fire and Icom chatter saying the Taliban were going to shoot an RPG; everyone cursing those fucking helicopter cowards for being unable to wait for just one more minute while we got our shit together. And me setting the camera down to shoot at two men sitting on a hill watching all this unfold while sipping chai, the first spectators in real time of what took place. Them there on the hill "haji-squatting," looking shady, probably too intrigued by our early morning catastrophe to move. Me, amazed that my rifle is actually able to muster off a few rounds, because I haven't cleaned or used it once during the entire deployment.

"Two guys on the hiilll . . ." I try to say, as my voice loses steam and tapers out, like my gun, which jams up, and I tap-rack-bang the thing over and over till I'm just smacking it, and smacking it again, trying to force some coherence and order into what is basically a shipwreck of a situation.

"Are you shooting?" the guys near me ask. They're popping off rounds over the wall at the compounds across the field without getting positive identification, some of them without even looking, just holding their rifles over the wall and spraying, our training having gone out the window.

I nod.

"Good," Boone says. "Anyone who's not a Marine, fucking kill them."

Did the guys on the hill have a weapon? I doubt it, but I don't think I was really trying to hit them so much as get them to go away. But they continued to sit there, as obstinate as ghosts. They say you feel as if you're leaving your body during times of extreme stress, but I think we felt more like we wanted to leave the confines of earthly physics so that we could kill whoever was shooting at us, whoever had gotten Bernhard; that we could jump up and join the helicopters circling above us, dropping gun runs that sounded like sawmills on the compounds across the field, and direct them with precision through sheer will. The helplessness of being grounded.

If you're watching you might wonder, "What are they shooting at? Where are they running to? Why was he on the roof to begin with?" Maybe a 3D animation of the day is needed, a total reconstruction of the compound and each shot that was fired. Is it possible that in a hundred years they'll be able to use the footage to expand the scope of view? To get a clearer shot of each moment, each passing second? Maybe rewind the clock and see the outcome of different scenarios, iterations of how that moment could have played out. In another hundred years will they be able to go inside and analyze the internal mechanisms grinding inside each of us? Will they be able to reconstruct the algorithm of Platt's anger and guilt through facial analysis as he says obstinately, "He got shot 'cause he was standing straight the fuck up. I told him once, stay low"?

Will they be able to feel the helplessness of Doc as he cried out, "Bernhard, no! Don't touch the bandages!" but Bernhard did so anyway because the synapses in his brain were not functioning and made his hand keep moving toward the wound like a bloody itch that couldn't be scratched, forcing Doc to reset the bandages for the third time? By the end of it they weren't even trying to keep them on anymore, and were fireman's-carrying his limp, dripping body like any other piece of equipment that needed to be evacuated at all costs.

Here's the thing: when you film a person dying, you carry the knowledge that you made them into a death symbol for the rest of your life. You killed them twice, and each time someone watches, you kill them again.

———

Once we'd finally medevaced Bernhard, after moving him three times to different places where the pilots finally felt safe enough to land, we walked home. Lieutenant Anderson changed out Doc's and Sabbagh's cammies, which were soaked in blood, and Elmira started scrubbing Bernhard's flak jacket. Some guys cried a little, others just sat there.

Doc came over to me shirtless, wearing only his trousers and a do-rag, asking to see the footage.

"You sure?" I asked.

"Yeah, lemme see it," he said.

I hadn't even dumped it onto my computer yet, so he sat and watched on the camera's viewfinder, a miniaturized version of something that still felt unreal.

"I can't hear anything," he said.

I grabbed some headphones and plugged them in for him and he watched silently, stopping occasionally to rewind, me pacing around next to him. I'm not sure what he was looking for, maybe a sign that he'd done his job as best a medic could, though I wasn't sure what more he could have done.

Over the years he'd find plenty of things he could have done differently, and the guilt we all felt was nothing compared to his obsessiveness, scanning through old Navy corpsman playbooks for how to treat a head wound, running through the procedures over and over, staring at manuals with crude, cereal-box-esque drawings of Marines bleeding out, until he was making his own playbook, locating the bullet still lodged in the back of Bernhard's head and conducting field neurosurgery, finally saving Bernhard, saving us all.

The next day, Platt led us to the same house. Back through the maze that now carried the stench of decay, to the end compound where we all felt the sickness crawling around inside us, like walking through a recently fumigated building. I kept expecting to see bloodstains on the ground, but they were gone.

"We've only got a fucking month left before we go home," some of the guys grumbled. What were we doing going back to the same place? What more could be achieved?

But Platt wanted payback. If Bernhard had seen the bad guys before he got shot, then that meant he could, too. Admittedly, we all wanted payback; it's just that Platt believed it was possible. He hoped there was still a chance to give the movie a happy ending. And, of course, he wanted me right by his side for it.

Lieutenant Anderson gave us the obligatory speech before we

stepped out, acknowledging the pain of our loss, but reminding us that we were fucking Marines and we had a fucking job to do. That was the gig, remember? The drudgery of combat, the nine-to-five of killing?

We set up in the death house again, but this time we brought all the squads as backup so we didn't feel so naked. We had guys positioned everywhere, providing overwatch, hidden deeper back in the maze, and, most importantly, air support on standby. For air to commit its limited resources they had to see that it was actually needed, and yesterday's debacle was enough for them to bring out all the big guns. Those of us with Platt's squad in the compound still felt the residuals of the day before, but now there was the emotional support that being surrounded by all that ass brought. The Taliban were probably still high off their win and feeling emboldened. Their victories were short, slick, and unverified, but I tend to think they built them up in their minds the same way we did.

They started by opening up on us with a couple of obligatory potshots to test the waters. We responded by calling in Excalibur missiles, not even bothering firing back with our own weapons. The shot got approved immediately, and landed like lightning, with delayed thunder coming a few seconds after the blast, the physicality of sound ever apparent.

Knox, a short, chubby SAW gunner, noted, "They go into space before they come down," and I filmed the cathartic joy on each member of Platt's squad's faces, as if God had decided to try to right his wrong from the day before.

"That's gotta be the most beautiful thing I've ever seen," Knox said.

As the blasts continued, the squads surrounding us started to open up in solidarity, dumping all their rounds into the same spot the missiles were landing, throwing everything we had at them, until, in the cacophony of destruction, we could feel Bernhard there with us. With each thud of missile impact, we grew back stronger from the day before, until the empty space in each of us was almost full again.

Afterward I lit a joint and we watched the sun go down. We talked about how Bernhard was still alive when we got him on the bird, and how they might be able to save him at the hospital in Germany. We congratulated ourselves for this achievement, in denial about the reality that, even if Bernhard were to survive, he'd most likely be permanently brain damaged, but no one was ready to think about whether that was better or worse.

Platt sat staring silently at the map of compounds in front of him, the word *compound* a misnomer, since after the day's action they were basically just pieces of broken, leftover wall. He looked up from the map and smiled at me. He announced that we would conduct a battle damage assessment that night to see how many of them we'd gotten, waiting for an hour when the Taliban wouldn't be able to spot us walking across the field to that other side of ourselves.

———

The rest happens in night vison just past my viewfinder. I've entered the frame as full-tilt cinema verité spectator, eyes unblinking, mind on autopilot. It's a lucid dream, one I suddenly realize I can stop at any time. But the thing is, I can't decide whether I want to wake up. I kind of want to see what's going to happen, so I let the movie play itself out.

The Taliban lack night vision; they're unable to turn the world inside out like we are. They're trapped by the limitations of their slumbering bodies, and as we walk stoned across the field, clumsy but invisible, to inspect for the bodies of killed enemies, our "battle damage assessment," our KIAs, I think about the Taliban sitting down for dinner over a small fire somewhere among the ruins. In the green infrared of the camera, which is my face, we see the boys moving across craters, through destroyed mud huts and over gentle, forgotten wadis, like the "jolly green giants" of Vietnam of yore, only this is not Vietnam, this is Helmand, and these are twenty-first-century fireflies, neon-lit soldiers taking their little war by storm.

When we get to the buildings across the field, we can still detect the smell of ozone, a remnant of the Excalibur missiles' trip above and back down to earth, like a scoop of celestial fro-yo, gas-flavored Creamsicle. Do they ever not want to come down? Drifting high enough that they lose gravitational pull, to then go roaming eternally through the galaxy, until the slight, vacuum-sealed *pop* of a muted space explosion. When we were little kids, we thought we could blow things up with our minds. I wonder how that translates to combat, if it validates the Me Generation's delusions. The way we gave ourselves agency while growing up in a society where technological changes and mass shootings were as on the rise as the sea level was to envision ourselves as the conduits of a more immediate destruction. We call in a bomb threat, then watch them evacuate the school. We call in an air strike and watch the movie explosions come to life.

The camera takes me sidewise into a three-walled compound. As it does so, the edges of the frame wobble a bit, a reminder that this is a false-flag operation, and that we made the war as palatable as possible for long enough. There in the corner is a still-breathing body. He is waiting for us. His breath crackles in the night vision. His blood is a stream of green pixels.

When revenge comes it is dull and quick, no feelings till later.

"Ey, we got one in here," someone calls.

"Oh, shit."

"Motherfucker."

Next to the man is a rifle, which was all the justification we ever needed. You, the participant whose name I can't mention for legal reasons, pick up the man's hand almost tenderly, as if to comfort him in his final moments.

"Stop hitting yourself, bro," you say, as you begin batting him in the face with it. The rest of us guffaw, and when we do, the camera gyrates ever so slightly. The man looks beleaguered. He knows his fate. Here this nameless man is Osama bin Laden, in this room, in my viewfinder. The ghost that hangs over it all, home and abroad. We finally found the video that is locked away somewhere in a Pentagon vault, where only those with the right security clearance, above top secret, into the ethers of the Special Access Program, are granted access. Where incongruent dreams the future can't articulate yet (Like why was bin Laden reading Noam Chomsky? Why was he reading *The New Pearl Harbor?*) are fully hashed out, and everything is illuminated. It's one of the perks of being a government ghoul; you get to watch the JFK assassination in Navy SEAL, Tier One operator GoPro glory. It's an initiation for those who make it high enough—NVG terrors that speak to our most entrenched patriotic fears, the knowledge that soon America will lose its hegemony, and then anything will be possible.

You look down at him for a moment before putting a bullet in his head, catching a few of us off guard, and we flinch because the sound is sharp, even through the silencer you put on.

"That's for Bernhard," you say.

The others take the silenced gun, and the bullets that can't be heard by anyone but us, unaccounted for in the war's twenty-year hail of gunfights, bombings, and air strikes, and swiftly plant more into the man's torso and head. Slowly, moving in with zero shake, a dolly shot, the Kino-Eye of my vision approaches and tilts down at the man who is almost not a face anymore but is somehow still able to smile, aware of the secret, the fact that, in the upper-right-hand corner of my screen, there is a blinking record icon that is not red.

I'm not recording.

"Hit record," I say inside the shell, but the words are warbled like underwater. "Hit record," but I can't because I have no arms or hands, and the frame extends past my torso down to my toes, and the world is a screen enveloping me in its monolith. It's like when I was a kid and I'd get vertigo staring at the TV too long, or like when my dad took me to see *Videodrome* when I was six and I had a panic attack. It's too late anyway. Like neon ghosts we've moved on, returning to the patrol base to share news of what we found to those we know will keep it hush-hush, a secretive celebration. I'm kicking myself because I missed that ever-so-elusive thing that is supposed to happen in war, the kill shot. There's the enemy—shoot 'em. But I'm also glad because it wasn't the right kind of kill.

And anyway, I still had the footage of Bernhard; I told myself I didn't need more deathcam atrocities. In my head we were still good guys; not "the" good guys, but still okay.

A couple of days later Lieutenant Anderson told us that Bernhard's mom had taken him off life support. This was the final death blow to our fantasy that we had saved Bernhard's life.

"I guess she wanted that hundred K," Platt said indignantly, referring to the $100,000 the military pays to the next of kin when their son or daughter dies.

"We weren't supposed to be in that compound in the first place," Derrickson said, in a side conversation that developed among the group that sheltered their own feelings of guilt and inadequacy. He didn't have the nerve to say it to Platt's face. None of us did. Guilt always needs a perp to share the blame. War is a constant game of deflection.

Either way, the jig was up. We went back out, but this time Platt took it easy. He sensed that many of us were done, that the game had cheated us by revealing it wasn't a game at all; that it was actually a bad joke and we were the punch line. He and Ali walked down to the river and talked about going swimming. Ali was happy for the first time. He saw that we wouldn't be waking up at 3 a.m. anymore to go run around like maniacs trying to win the war all by ourselves. We walked by a house where a man and his wife were outside making bread, and we all coaxed Ali into asking him for some. The man tore us a few pieces and handed them out to us, still warm and moist as we bit into them, but when his wife saw, she started berating him. They barely had enough food for themselves and he was giving them out to us like *we* were the charity cases? Didn't we have our own food? she asked. Weren't *they* the ones who were supposed to be starving? Ali tried to give the bread back, but the man refused. The rest of us continued to eat, relishing the treat. Because fuck 'em anyway, right? We were done playing nice.

Platt and I made plans for when we would do the final interview for the piece. The Bernhard footage was burning a hole in my hard drive. Years later I would wish that I'd never filmed the thing, after I'd grown up and stopped being a Marine; but if you're a scumbag before you get in uniform, you're even more a scumbag till you get out. And my initial feelings about filming Bernhard's death were that of secret pride. I knew what I had recorded was "powerful," but at the time its power derived from my own personal greed, the compulsion to capture the "true cost of war" at any cost to the people involved, the kind of imagery that defines a generation of soldiers and elevates mere point-and-shooters into artists. The Larry

Clark moment had found me. It would be a while before that glitzy pretense could come down.

———

We found a nice mud hut to do the interview in, and Platt sat down and sighed heavily once he saw the red light glow "on" in front of him. Platt was an orator of great magnitude, bridging the swagger of John Wayne with the contemporary good ol' boy attitude of Bradley Cooper.

"This area we're in," he drawled. "It's bad. It extends from Padigzy down to Husan's Village. With us here, we're basically the last defense for the rest of the battalion, and we've been holding it down all by ourselves."

I had no idea what he was talking about saying we were the last defense, and I wondered if he was just making it up or had pulled it from some well of knowledge I'd never been given access to. But it sounded good, like something people could articulate back home, the "we're the victims out here, we're outnumbered" type of American counterlogic that translated to Academy Award–nominated masturbations about the brotherhood of war. "The last defense" before total annihilation, like Marcus Luttrell's fake story *Lone Survivor*, where he wrote of two hundred Taliban fighters that overtook his squad, when it was actually only seven or eight.

Eventually I asked Platt about Bernhard.

"You replay it over and over in your mind," he said. "Maybe I should have taken him off the roof, but . . . you know, we needed those eyes up there to protect the squad." He looked down at the floor and shook his head. "Just a tough day. Bird kept coming in and taking off because the LZ [landing zone] was too hot. Ended up having to carry him on my back about five hundred meters to a new location."

I nodded, not realizing at the time that Platt had never carried Bernhard once during the whole ordeal. It seemed like an insignificant detail anyway, and it was perfectly fine with me if Platt wanted to play hero for the piece. That's why I had been following him around to begin with. But the lie of it all would grow in his mind, and would carry unexpected consequences for him down the road.

I put the video together to send to Chief Warrant Officer Walsh, the car salesman back at Camp Leatherneck who was in charge of releasing all of our footage. This video was to be my magnum opus, a ten-minute-long mini-documentary about the whole operation, starting with the helo insert (minus the door gunner trying to break my camera), moving into the terrain and the challenges it presented, a brief segment about the Marines' relationship with Ali and what a valuable asset he was, and ending with the medevac of Bernhard, which took up most of the video. The somber closing note would remind people back home that we were dying out here. I burned it to a disk, wrapped it in MRE cardboard to safeguard it, put it on the next convoy that came across the river, and waited with glee and suspense for it to go viral like the other videos I had made.

But days went by and it still hadn't been released. I emailed Walsh to see what was up, but he didn't get back to me. I started to worry that the disk hadn't reached him. I burned another one and sent it out again.

It was around this time that Daniels, our dog handler, stepped on an IED.

We had been steering clear of the maze at this point, after the bombings, and so the enemy figured they would have to come to us. They started planting IEDs everywhere. Elmira was leading his squad around the AO, occasionally calling in their position back to the PB, sort of half plodding about, half killing time, when

Daniels's bomb-sniffing dog smelled a hit. They put up a cordon, expecting it to be a false positive, because bomb-sniffing dogs were about as reliable at finding IEDs as groundhogs were at predicting the coming winter. The dog lay down in a spot in the dirt, indicating where the IED was, and Daniels would follow with his minesweeper. The thing went off like crazy and he called back to the others, telling them to keep their distance, not seeing that the dog had already lain down in another spot, indicating a second IED he had not yet seen. The others saw the smoke go up and felt the air push them apart, rattling their brains like egg yolks inside shells of skull. The dog was eviscerated and Daniels was flipped upside down, both of them lost forever in the clumsiness of our occupation. I've heard people say an IED hit is like slipping on a banana peel, only when you come down everything is gone.

As an act of courtesy to Doc Coleman, Elmira called in Doc Lee over the radio, our other corpsman, who was busy at the time playing slap bets with Knox, and told him to get the fuck over there. Daniels's right leg was still attached except for a shredded chunk of inner thigh. His left leg was completely gone, and he began to freak out a little as the guys were working on him.

"My balls," he kept saying. "They good?"

Elmira reached down, took off Daniels's protective blast diaper, and grinned. Those things we hated wearing because it was like walking around with a catheter, that the command forced us to wear because too many guys were killing themselves after getting their nuts blown off, had actually worked. Elmira grabbed hold of Daniels's reproductive organs and squeezed hard, Daniels letting out a scream of relief before he blacked out for a bit. When Lee got there, he started to freak out, too; it was his first IED hit, the first real casualty he'd had to treat. Elmira took Lee aside, holding him by the shoulders and looking him dead in the eye.

"Do your fucking job."

"All right, yeah," Lee said, and he jumped into it, patching Daniels up and applying tourniquets as best he could before the medevac came. Believe it or not, these were the small victories that we came home with and that we could live with, the knowledge that we did our jobs when the moment came down to it. Everyone had a job to do, and the smaller your part was, the less you came back with. My problem was that my job was *too* insignificant. Combat Camera didn't serve the group in any real way, other than to occasionally beef them up and catalog the things many of us would, with time, want to forget. And, of course, there was the sneaking suspicion that my presence had actually caused certain things to happen, bad things that would make the others come to regret their invitations to let me in.

The next day Lieutenant Anderson told me I had to go. Walsh had been calling a bunch of people telling them to get me on the first convoy out of there.

"What's up, sir?" I asked Lieutenant Anderson.

"Christmas," he said. "They want you to go around getting shout-outs from every guy in the unit so they can play them during the Macy's parade or something."

"Seriously?"

"Apparently."

I sensed what was really going on. Walsh had seen the Bernhard video and didn't want me filming anymore.

"Did he say anything about the video I sent him? Why hasn't he released it?"

Lieutenant Anderson shrugged. "We'll miss you, YouTube. Make sure you get shout-outs from all the guys here before you leave."

I felt like I was being orphaned off. These were my guys now; I couldn't leave them out there with no one to record them. Their disasters and pseudo victories were mine, too, their struggles and complaints had been fully internalized by me; I'd find myself mimicking the same things they were saying. I felt I was one of them even though I'd only been with them for a couple of weeks, and I cursed that POG Walsh for being unable to see the bigger picture, the important work I was doing.

But in the squad's eyes, the deployment was largely over. I spoke with Sabbagh and Knox before I left.

"I just wanna go home, man. I think we all do at this point."

"Yeah," Knox concurred. "Fucking Platt needs to chill."

"We did what we had to do, I guess. Like, let's get the fuck out of here already. I mean who really wants to get their legs blown off a month before we go home?"

"Bernhard only had four months left on his contract. They had to extend it so he could come out here."

We all shook our heads thinking about it.

"At least we got that guy across the field," I said after a minute. They both looked at me.

"You heard about that?" Sabbagh asked.

"I was there," I said.

"You were?" he asked. "I thought you came back with us after the air strikes."

"Yeah, after we did the battle damage assessment."

"Third squad did a BDA," Knox said. "It was ▮▮▮▮ who found the guy and shot him."

"I almost filmed it," I said. "But obviously I didn't."

"You're trippin', YouTube," Sabbagh said. "You need to lay off the hash."

"Yeah, and keep that shit on the DL," Knox said. "Pretty sure they, like, violated the Geneva Conventions or some shit."

I started feeling my mind drift away like dead leaves down a drainage ditch, and me chasing after them. Were they fucking with me or was I fucking with myself? Why was the vision I had so strong, yet so grossly cinematic? Why hadn't I recorded it?

Platt asked if I could give him a copy of the video I made that hadn't been released yet, as well as his entire interview before I left.

"You gotta do something with this someday," he said, watching himself on camera as he spat a giant wad of tobacco juice on the floor, enthralled by his own stories of the trials and tribulations of being a Marine squad leader.

"It's like controlling chaos," he was saying in the vid. "Controlled chaos."

"Otherwise," he said, "no one will know what happened."

I promised him I would, knowing that whatever I did would probably not be his cup of tea, and would not show Platt in the light he had seen himself in and wanted others to see. As I got on the boat to ferry us across the river, I felt like something dirty had been planted inside me. I filmed the young boy pulling the rope that brought the overturned car to our side of the shore. He did that thing Afghans do where they stare directly into the camera forever, like it was some kind of contest, until I stopped and put it away.

CHAPTER 11

Erasing the River

I teamed back up with Loya to film the Christmas shout-outs, and we talked for hours about what we'd seen. I told him about Bernhard and Daniels, and showed him all the awesome things I'd recorded. The bombings, the firefights, the bloopers, etc. I never mentioned the wounded man we killed or the old guy they beat up, because, with each passing day, it felt like those things were par for the course given what we'd gone through, and I didn't want to be some kind of buzzkill.

Loya had been hashed out the entire time I was gone. He'd spent his days in a part of the AO where there was such little action that the Marines there didn't even need to stand post most of the time. This was disappointing, considering that the best footage he'd gotten was of them hanging out with the Afghan police, hacking to death chickens they'd bought at a local shop to eat for dinner each night. I couldn't be too upset about it, though—Loya was nervous because they'd given the entire battalion a piss test while I was across the river. It was real shady shit; they waited till the end of the deployment to administer the only urinalysis, when everyone was feeling most complacent. Lewis, being the sweetheart that he was, had given him a clean sample in a 5-hour Energy bottle to pour into the urinalysis cup when the time came, but Loya had lost his nerve.

"The staff sergeant was staring right at my dick the whole time," he lamented.

"I'm sure you'll be good, they only test like a quarter of the samples," I said. It was how the Marine Corps kept things in balance. If they tested every sample, then half the battalion would probably come up positive. "Plus, we're all sweating and burning so much fat out here that even if they did test yours, you'd be clean."

He thought about this, then nodded. "Yeah, you're probably right. I mean, hopefully. Fuck."

Our unit was gearing up to rotate out, and the unit that was replacing us was starting to send forward attachments to get a lay of the land before all their guys came out. Everyone was getting fat off old care packages that had finally reached us after months held up in transit, tearing through stale gingerbread cookies and canned Vienna sausages while dreaming about America and family—building up our return to the point of sublimity. Loya and I went around filming the highs on their faces, the crow's-feet of deployment creasing around their eyes, like strange light-up toys beginning to flicker in the dark.

One guy could barely hold back the emotions and kept repeating himself. "Hi, honey," he said during his shout-out. "I . . . I miss you, and . . . I miss you, Nicole. I love you . . . I . . . Hi, baby . . . I . . ."

"You want to try that again?" I asked, but the guy just shook his head and walked away before I could see the tears coming.

Another kept talking about how his girlfriend had spent nearly all his deployment money and then broken up with him in a "dear John," sent just a few weeks ago.

"How much do you have left?" one of his buddies asked in the background while I was filming him.

" 'Bout two grand," he said.

"Jee-*zuss*!" the buddy cried. "You know what you should do when you get back? Slash her tires. Fuckin' go to her house at night while she's asleep, and slash her fuckin' tires, dude." Then he looked over at me. "You're not recording this, are you?"

———

I knew I should be across the river, not filming this bullshit. I was also certain that these videos wouldn't be able to air during any kind of parade back home. They liked cleaner versions of "the boys," soldiers who looked like they'd showered and had a hot meal in the past week; sailors and airmen who'd probably spoken to their wives via satellite phone just the other day, not the unshaven messes these guys were, cut off from society, huddled outside of mud huts chain-smoking cigarettes and talking about slashing their girlfriends' tires.

Walsh still hadn't released my opus video, but I'd finally gotten ahold of him via email. He said I would need to come back to Camp Leatherneck to re-edit it. Loya and I rushed through the rest of the shout-outs and made our way back to the FOB. Having not showered in months, we were greeted by our commanding officer with an initial step back.

"Look at these two combat hobos!" he said, clapping us on the back, then wiping his hand discreetly. He and some other Public Affairs officers were watching the movie *Elf* on a big-screen projector in their office. It felt weird to be in an air-conditioned room with white walls and plastic everywhere. "And Mr. CNN himself," he said, beaming at me. The rest of the officers gave us a round of applause.

"That video you shot was a game changer," one of them said, shaking my hand. "It looked like the OK Corral out there with those guys popping up out of that cliff wall."

"Yes, sir. The cliff wall," I said. The empty cliff wall we wasted about 100,000 rounds of ammunition on.

"It wasn't just the combat footage, though. It was the interviews you conducted. What was that line their lieutenant said?"

"You hear about people being battle-tested," Walsh said, reciting it from memory. "Well, this one tested the boys."

"This one tested the boys.... And that thousand-yard stare he had. Woof, it gave me chills."

Loya and I looked at each other. These guys had been in Afghanistan for almost a year yet they still had the same delusions about war they'd probably had when they were kids. The myth was still strong in their hearts, and you couldn't blame them. You almost felt bad for them, sitting here at Camp Leatherneck in their little bubble, coming up with stories they could tell when they got home that wouldn't make their wives suspect they'd had it harder back home than the Fobbits did out here.

That line Lieutenant Gandy had used in the video was a good one, though, straight out of the officer's handbook. I once heard a lieutenant talking about OCS—Officer Candidate School—and how he first knew they were all full of shit when one of his instructors was giving a class about how to give speeches to young Marines heading into battle.

"Be calm, collected, and always stand straight," the instructor had said. "Then, just before you begin, I want you to turn and imagine a camera right there, off to the side, recording everything you're about to say."

I asked Walsh about the video of the river crossing, but he told me to wash up and get some chow first. "We'll get into that later," he said.

We showered in one of the portable heads on the giant base, scrubbing our blackened hands raw with little success; the dirt was so ingrained that it would only come out after our skin had shed it weeks later. One of the ComCam guys who worked at the TIPS (Tactical Imagery Processing System) gave me some time alone. I called my parents for the first time and told them I'd be coming home soon, but asked them not to come to North Carolina for the homecoming ceremony because I'd see them in New York during my deployment leave anyway. Then Loya and I headed to the Morale, Welfare, and Recreation Center, where they had internet, and we created OkCupid accounts with the idea that we'd have a whole host of women lined up waiting for us upon our return. We really thought people would give a shit that we were coming back from the war.

"You think I should use this one?" I asked him, showing off a picture of me smiling while bleeding from my head after the grenade attack. We didn't have any normal photos of us to use, so we were pulling stills from the footage we'd shot during the operation.

"Oh, shit," he said.

"Yeah, oh, shit," I said.

"You *gotta* use that. You'll get some serious sympathy responses."

The only message I got was from another Marine asking why I was using a fake photo to look like I'd actually been in combat. "Are you so much of a pog that you have to use fake pictures to make yourself feel like a real Marine to try to get pussy??" he wrote. Laughing face emoji, laughing face emoji.

The next morning we went to Walsh's office, where he sat smiling at us like we were his prized possessions. He'd recently been promoted, and I think a large part of it was because of the work we'd done during the operation.

"You said I'd need to re-edit the video of the river crossing, sir?" I asked.

"Yup, yup. You're gonna have to take out all the shots of the Marine that was killed," he said, as if it was no biggie at all. I had been expecting this, but not quite as nonchalantly as he was delivering it to me.

"Why?" I said, the quiver in my voice giving myself away.

"Well, for one thing," Walsh said, "it's *way* too graphic, and more importantly, the family of the Marine—"

"Noah Bernhard."

"Right. Lance Corporal Bernhard's family has to be informed of his death first before we can show anything depicting that whole episode."

"What are you talking about? His mom pulled the plug on him. He's been dead for weeks. How did you not know that?"

Loya glanced at me.

"Look," Walsh said. "This is how it's gonna go: if you want that video released, you have to take out every shot of him, both during the medevac and before, when he was still alive. There's still some great footage in there we can use."

I scoffed. "Before he got shot, too? So now he just doesn't exist, I guess." I turned to Loya because looking at Walsh's slicked-back hair and doughy face was making me want to kick a hole in his desk. "He never existed, right? Gotta erase him. He never existed. I guess, uh, I should just delete the whole thing, then. We never even went across the river to begin with, right?"

The river had become everything in my mind. It had morphed and grown to epic proportions. It was the Kajaki Dam we were supposed to be securing, it was the school we built that killed all those kids, it was those fat, stupid surveillance blimps in the sky that I now felt like I was tethered to, floating higher and higher with each newfound source of indignation. I felt so fucking self-righteous I thought I might hurl.

Loya got me out of there before I could do or say something that would get me court-martialed. To Walsh's credit, it wasn't his decision to cut the footage. A general had seen it and said "no way," but I'm sure Walsh didn't put up a fight. I don't even think they archived it; it served no purpose to the mission of Combat Camera. We were supposed to show that things were winding down, that we were handing the country over to the ANA. Dead Marines didn't fit that narrative.

Somewhere it occurred to me that never once on the news had I seen a U.S. soldier dead or dying in Afghanistan. They showed dead Iraqis and Afghans strewn like trash in the streets; they showed graphic footage of police shootings all the time; car accidents and other "disturbing" images played on a loop 24/7, but the American soldier was still sacred.

I re-edited the video, taking out every shot of Bernhard, and Walsh would scrub through it and find frames where the camera shook, and, in the shake, at the edge of the frame, there he would be, lying bleeding on the ground, and I'd have to go back in and remove it. He also made me take out the portion with Ali, because it was too long, and had me end the video with Sergeant Lopez high-fiving another guy after we'd blown up a Taliban bunker.

"You have that pride about you," Platt said in his interview. "'Cause they sent you across the river so you know that they trust you."

"We did what we had to do out here," Lopez said as a closing remark. "We made a name for 1/6 Weapons Company."

People watching wouldn't have a clue what we were doing or why, which, when you thought about it, was pretty accurate. It made absolutely no sense. It didn't really matter anyway; we were going home. I couldn't stay too upset because I still had the raw footage tucked safely away in my hard drives.

When the rest of the unit got to the FOB, Loya, Matty, and I drank Robitussin cough syrup together again, even though we'd sworn we wouldn't. We got lost and ended up near the Danish Army side of the base, where they had a volleyball court and a pastry shop. One of the Danish soldiers sat down with us and asked what part of the war we were coming from.

"Sangin and Kajaki," we told him. He gave us a very sympathetic nod. Loya got up and puked next to the volleyball court. We confessed that we had each drank three bottles of cough syrup.

"I knew you guys were fucked up on something," he said. "I just couldn't figure out what."

Later we tried to convince Matty to be in our movie when we got home. His mom lived in New Jersey, so he could come into New York with us when we were filming the subway scenes. That was still important to us for some reason, taking mushrooms on the subway. I envisioned us walking along the tracks to the old abandoned stations we used to go to when I was in high school. A kid I knew had gotten hit by a train while trying to tag one of them up with graffiti, and I guess that had stayed with me. It was very cinematic. My friends liked to mention him as if he was a close and dear pal, though I only remember meeting him once. His death made us feel like real New York kids—old Johnny who got killed while graffitiing in the subway. It was starting to feel like the Marines had saved me from a similar dumb fate. When you're young, needless death is the only way to go. The myths of our former selves.

Matty laughed at our proposal. He had changed during his time with the snipers and wanted nothing to do with our movie. He was professional now. Apparently that video I had recorded, now titled "ONE SHOT ONE KILL" on YouTube, had given the snipers a lot of grief because the guys in it weren't wearing their proper gear or something. Never mind the Nazi SS symbol, or the fact that I'd edited out the extra shots they'd fired. Matty also told me to delete any videos that might show him smoking hash. I pleaded, trying to convince him of why they were some of the most important moments from the whole deployment—his big, shit-eating grin captured everything about being twenty years old in Afghanistan— but he wouldn't have it.

"Do you guys not realize that your actions have consequences?" he scolded. "Do you know how much trouble we could get in if that stuff ever got out?" He seemed even more paranoid than before. Of course, within the hour he'd have me record him as he delivered some kind of public service announcement to America, how they had no idea what we'd gone through and would never be able to repay us for our sacrifices. "America," he said, dripping with Robitussin-fueled grandeur and condescension, "I almost feel bad for you. You don't know how good you all have it." He drifted in and out like a drunken sailor, his arm crooked around Loya's neck. "But I'll forgive you, America. We're coming home."

Later that night, in an offhanded way, he said, "I know for a fact we committed war crimes, but whatever."

There was no need to press him on this; we all knew that Scout Snipers could be pretty cold-blooded. Just a few weeks ago a squad from another unit deployed to Musa Qala had posted a video of themselves urinating on three dead Taliban they killed. People back home were having a minor freak-out about it. The uniform is a monolith for Americans abroad—one bad photo or video can confirm their fears about the ugliness of themselves, or it can negate all their doubts and make them feel like the benevolent souls they desire. But it's always one or the other; saints or sinners.

The thing that always pissed me off about snipers was their over-confidence in their belief that they alone were the ones protecting everyone else. They got furious when their shots weren't approved. "I'm watching a dude with a bag full of rifles just walking around, and they tell me I don't have positive identification," one of them complained to me after a night observation mission gone wrong. There was always something in the way, some misguided hurdle from the command that prevented them from killing more people.

I thought back to that day on the hill, and how eager I had been to be with them as they took the shot. How much did my desire to film them in action influence their desire to shoot someone?

When I went to see Platt and the rest of the guys from the river to explain why the video had been so drastically cut down, they looked sad to see me. "You didn't hear?" they asked. Platt had stepped on an IED their last week out there, cutting him in half and severing both of his legs up to the hip. He had been taking them through the maze one last time. They said he was weirdly calm when they medevaced him, was still giving them orders, reminding them that they'd have to take all of his ammo before he could get on the bird. The blast had broken his spine, so he couldn't look up to see if his legs were gone, and the others had lied and told him he was good. He was currently in Germany, in a coma but stable. Also, he was being written up for an award. That was the thing that made it okay, I thought. He would be happy about that.

"We shot a guy on a motorcycle," Sabbagh told me. "We hit his gas tank and he went up in flames. You should have been recording that, man." And then the gnawing, grating feeling of having missed something, in this case a real kill shot in full deathcam glory, was back. Even though it might not have happened exactly the way that they said.

———

Loya and I began piecing together the prime cuts from our footage; the best "kinetic" scenes, the best downtime scenes, the best moments that captured that ridiculous thing we still envisioned as the theme of the movie: war as an adventure, war as shock value, war as a heightened experience for American men trying to discover the truth of their bodies and minds. You know, *White boy wasted. Finna go buck wild.*

We got set to board the plane to Germany, then Ireland, then home feeling as invincible as rock stars and more vulnerable than leaves. The footage was safe, our memories preserved. Our psyches could be dealt with later, once we'd drunken ourselves into a stupor.

They called a formation a few days before we were set to leave and read off a list of people to go talk to the first sergeant. Loya was on it. His urinalysis had come back positive. He would be held in the brig when we got back to North Carolina, then they'd probably kick him out of the military with no benefits. But first they'd keep him a while to think about how badly he'd fucked up.

My first thought was selfish, a feeling of terror at being unable to complete the movie. Then I saw the look on Loya's face, heard the subtle dread in his voice when he told me in his usual unrushed tone that he'd already told his mom and dad to come to the "heroes' homecoming" at Camp Lejeune. He lay back in his cot and looked up at the ceiling. I couldn't tell if he wanted to cry. All I could do was feed him some optimism mixed with outrage.

"They'll never be able to use those urinalyses in court, man," I said. "How the fuck can they piss-test us in a war zone? We patrol through poppy fields every day. We eat food the locals give us that could be laced with opium—how do we know? That's what you should say, dude."

When we asked Lewis, he agreed that this seemed like a good defense, though I could tell he was hiding some skepticism, laced with a bit of I-told-you-so-ness. Either way, we built it up in our minds as Loya's get-out-of-jail-free card, the same way we'd built the war up, the same way we'd built the movie up, the same way we were now building our idea of home up.

CHAPTER 12

Keep Me Safe

The police in Jacksonville, North Carolina, were put on notice whenever an infantry unit was set to return from Afghanistan. Jacksonville, referred to by Marines sarcastically as "J-Vegas," was home to Camp Lejeune, the second-largest Marine base in the country. When I was there, the city consisted of disparate swaths of barbershops, tattoo parlors, and strip clubs, and a decrepit "Downtown" area that was mostly boarded-up shops and a lone bank that was only open certain days; the skeleton crew working there looked like they expected you to hold the place up whenever you walked in. An old forgotten canal that ran through the neighborhood was filled with waste. The town was surrounded by backwoods swamps and trailer parks that skirted the red zone of where our artillery units practiced their howitzer rounds. The cops and everyone else there hated us, but they were also dependent on us for their economy.

It was a hologram town, a gross, incestuous place, where the strip clubs looked like Walgreens with no windows, built temporarily with another place in mind, and where the dancers were mostly casualties of failed military marriages, women who were left in Jacksonville with no money and nowhere else to go, hell-bent on hustling the men who had hustled them.

It was a constant balancing act for the cops; if they gave out DUIs and disorderly conducts to everyone who warranted them, then the base would look bad, like the Marine Corps had a drinking problem. But they also had a quota to fill, so they would set up DUI checkpoints on Fridays and Saturdays outside the entrance to the base, only breathalyzing the guys who were so drunk they could barely hold on to the wheel. We had our own quotas to fill; endless quotas of sex, fighting, and beer to make up for lost time. Our eyes were like pinballs darting from one debaucherous scheme to the next. Where could we release our pent-up emotions without too many unnecessary casualties? Where could we go that the women didn't hate us? Where could we cry and berate taxi drivers and express our love for each other without being judged too harshly by the locals?

Before we were able to see our families, they went through our bags with bomb-sniffing dogs because some dickhead from the past had once tried to smuggle an AK-47 and a hand grenade back with him. Then they drove us to the base, where hundreds of family members were ready with waving signs and tear-streaked mascara, going apeshit for their beloved vets. It felt strange to see such a joyous occasion play out in front of a place that we all hated so much, just outside our barracks on Camp Lejeune, where most of our time was spent drinking and getting yelled at, doing PT at five in the morning still drunk, conducting drunk field days, etc. In the midst of them all stood a small woman with a button nose looking around anxiously. I made my way through the crowd of hugs and squeals and went up to her.

"Are you Loya . . . I mean, Justin's mom?" I asked.

She looked up at me fearing the worst. She began to speak as Loya's dad came over to join her. "Are you Miles? Justin told me about you. Where is he? We only spoke on the phone once before you came back and he wouldn't tell me what was happening."

Shit, I thought. Loya hadn't told her yet. I tried to explain that she couldn't see him because he was awaiting nonjudicial punishment and would probably be put on restriction.

"What does that *mean*?" she asked. "We came all the way from Texas." Her eyes started filling with tears. "Please just tell me what's happening. Where is Justin?" I scratched my head and looked around. She was going to find out eventually. I pointed out the battalion sergeant major to her, a jacked old guy who looked like Mr. Clean if he had sleeve tattoos on both arms. He would be the one to dole out whatever punishment befell Loya, but right now he was chatting with other families, talking about how great their sons had done on the deployment and how proud he was of all of us.

Loya's mom went over to him and demanded to see her son. The sergeant major was adamant that there was nothing he could do, but there's only so long you can maintain the impenetrable wall of Marine Corps bureaucracy in front of a crying mother pleading to see her son. Eventually he walked past the watching crowd of onlooking families and ducked into the S-3 building to retrieve a depleted-looking Loya. We stood around as his mom hugged him and wept. It felt like we were kids in school, and Loya had gotten expelled, except we had been getting shot at and killing people for the past seven months. And instead of going home, Loya was about to descend into another form of hell. Fifteen or so minutes later, the sergeant major took him back to his holding cell.

"Miles, I'm just going to ask," his dad said, pulling me aside. "Did he do it?"

I thought long on how to answer. What fantasies and delusions did we need to hold up and what could come down? I told him no, that there must have been some mistake with the drug test they gave us. He looked relieved; what's one more delusion when you're living the dream?

It wouldn't be for another six months, after the paperwork and everything was completed for him to get kicked out with a "bad conduct discharge," that he would be able to go home and see them again.

During that time, I made sure to visit him in his room every day, which he wasn't allowed to leave except to go to chow and to check in with the person on duty. Lewis came by one day while I was giving Loya a haircut and told us about a dream he'd been having. Lewis's contract was up in a few weeks and he would be leaving the Marines. He told us he dreamed he'd gotten out and gone to college, but was immediately arrested for a murder he didn't remember committing.

"Could this be some kind of separation anxiety?" we asked him. "You're worried about who you're going to be and what you're going to do when you get out." He said he couldn't wait to get out, so that didn't really hold up. We thought about it. The obvious thing, which we had subconsciously suppressed, was the fact that we had taken part in the state-sanctioned mass murder of a people we'd viewed as either amusing, hostile, or target practice. The discomfort Lewis was feeling meant he was actually the sanest and most humane out of all of us. He would be all right.

Many of the guys from the unit had decided they were about done with the Marine Corps; they couldn't wait the months or years left that they had on their contracts, and some of them started trying to get medically discharged for insanity so they could get out early.

Others didn't need to try; they were already going crazy. Boone, for instance, the boulder-like behemoth who had been Platt's right-hand man during the deployment, was being prescribed just about every antidepressant, antipsychotic, antihuman sleeping medication available to twenty-first-century man to get over his memories of what had happened to Bernhard and Platt. On top of this he was smoking Spice on the reg and was getting funny feelings about the way his wife was looking at him. Sergeant Elmira, who noticed Boone talking to himself during formations, tried to see if he was still reachable in the strange, heady space he now occupied since we'd gotten back. They were at Elmira's house drinking when he confronted him, and, in response, Boone inexplicably accused Elmira of fucking his wife. This infuriated Elmira, and there was a big scene with Elmira kicking him out, then pulling him out of his car because he was too fucked up to drive, then trying to get a cab for him before losing him somewhere in the woods, and finally saying fuck it and just going to bed, hoping he wouldn't show up again.

Boone's wife, who was now catching the drift, left town shortly thereafter to go stay with her parents. After she left, Boone went to medical half-naked and sobbing, and the medical officer there took a look at the list of pills he was on and decided to cut him off every one of them right there. A few days later he took off to his in-laws' with a case of Jack Daniel's, some lighter fluid, and a handgun. Luckily, they weren't home when he showed up—he might have killed them all, including himself—but he still burned their house to the ground. Big men are capable of big things when they're upset.

Incredibly, through some kind of liability loophole, the military determined it was the fault of the MO (medical officer) who'd taken him off all his meds. Instead of a dishonorable discharge, he was medically retired from the military with full honors. When someone showed me his mug shot from after he burned the house down, it was like I was meeting him for the first time. I had never once seen Boone's eyes; he was always wearing sunglasses during the deployment. Behind the façade his face was sad and boyish, a big angry toddler set loose with no custodian.

Matty saw Boone's luck as a sign of encouragement. Having become increasingly paranoid and disillusioned with the command, he told me he couldn't wait another day; he wanted out now. He'd come to a conclusion about the higher-ups. "They're just *insecure*," he told me, like he'd learned a new word. "They don't have what it takes to make it in the real world, and they know deep down that they're all fucked up, but they're too insecure. So, they take it out on us." On top of this, he'd gotten a girl back home pregnant and needed to get out so he could make things right with her, along with another girl he was seeing on the side.

He got focused, or thought he had, and went to see the Wizard, as we called the top shrink on base. There he went on and on about one of the snipers he knew whose legs had gotten blown off, to no effect. It was the Wizard's job to call bullshit on everyone claiming to be too crazy to continue their service, and Matty had gone in a little too hot, acting like he didn't know whether he was in Afghanistan or Camp Lejeune or Calcutta. The Wizard caught him off guard by pulling rank on him.

"Excuse me, Corporal," he said, stopping Matty mid–psychotic rant. "I want to remind you that you're talking to a colonel in the United States Marines, and I would appreciate it if you'd address me as such."

Matty didn't acknowledge this, instead turning around slowly in his chair to look blankly at the wall behind him. "I . . . I keep seeing his stumps sticking up in the air, after the smoke cleared. . . ."

The colonel's voice grew sterner this time, adding with it the weight of administrative action, and it compounded the severity of what Matty was trying to do. "I said, *you're talking to a colonel, shithead.*"

That's when some remnant of boot camp brainwashing kicked in, and out of Matty's mouth came a reluctant "Aye, sir."

The Wizard smiled tenderly. "You see, Corporal?" he said. "If you were really experiencing psychosis, my rank would have no meaning to you. It would have no bearing on your reality, because the definition of psychosis is a total disconnection from reality." He prescribed him a low dosage of Seroquel, which we decided to take recreationally, and which made my knees buckle and my heart flutter any time I yawned, for about a week straight.

Matty lamented the experience a few days later. He was snorting bath salts now to lift him up out of the Seroquel fog, and I took notice of his unkempt attire and the slight, drifty aberration of his right eye, which told me to keep my distance. The act was becoming reality.

A few nights later he was with Sax and another kid and they were lost somewhere outside the base, driving through the cold winter roads that surrounded Lejeune, amid the loggers working to clear the woods for more training exercises. To them it didn't look anything like the area near the base; it looked alien and otherworldly, because of the bath salts and the fact that they'd been binge-watching *Ancient Aliens* on the History Channel for two weeks straight. Sax abruptly stopped the car, because he said the cleared woods were beautiful and looked like a landing strip for ancient spacecraft, and the other kid opened his door and rolled out of his seat onto the frozen asphalt, where he lay for a while staring at and inhaling the exhaust fumes coming out from under the car. Matty was the first to say that this wasn't a good look for them, to be stopped on the side of the road like this. Sax agreed, but he also wanted to get on the other kid's level first, just to see if there was something there, and he went under the car with him to check it out. They were both lying under the car inhaling its fumes and feeling a strange warmth together, with Matty peering out of the window nervously, when an MP heading back to base noticed them and pulled over. Like a flash, Matty was up and out of the car into the dark woods, stripping off his clothes for good effect, bath salts and wanting out having got the better of him, pushing him into a new dimension. *You want crazy? Here I am.*

I'm up, they see me, I'm down, he repeated in his head while he ran, the old boot camp ditty they taught us to do when running toward the enemy. Helicopters, he told me. There were helicopters flying overhead looking for him. The MPs found him and brought him back to the base, and he was put in drug counseling for a couple of weeks, then kicked out with an other-than-honorable discharge.

He's a devout Christian now and hasn't returned my calls in years.

I was beginning to see that the infantry was an unhealthy group to remain around, and poor Loya was stuck there surrounded by all of them. As if it wasn't bad enough, during his check-ins with the Marine on duty, he'd been getting harassed by a lieutenant who was also on restriction and awaiting court-martial for stockpiling IEDs. During the deployment, he'd made his platoon hoard caches of weapons and bomb-making material that they found, then he'd plant them on Afghans he suspected of working for the Taliban. He felt the command wasn't letting him detain enough people, guys he knew—really knew, with the dumb certainty of someone who thinks they've seen it all—were bad guys. This went on for a while until one of his own corporals reported him up the chain of command. Now he was in the same boat as Loya, but still somehow feeling superior. He got into it with him one day while they were both waiting for the Marine on duty to check them off.

"What you on restriction for?" he asked in a high-pitched wheeze. The guy was only five foot four. I saw him once taunting an Afghan by whispering "Allahu akbar" in his ear repeatedly while their translator questioned him.

"Popped on the piss test, sir," Loya said.

"Here or over there?"

"Over there."

The lieutenant shook his head. "Heinous," he said. "Getting high with the ANA while you're supposed to be having your Marines' backs. That shit is fuckin'... *heinous*."

Loya just nodded.

"What's your MOS?" he asked.

"Combat Camera."

"Figures. Why they even let y'all come with us on deployments is a mystery. It's just a liability."

"Weren't you caught stockpiling IEDs, sir?" Loya said.

This really pissed the guy off. "I'm not legally allowed to discuss that, but let's just say I was looking out for my Marines, something you clearly wouldn't understand." He got up and told the Marine on duty he was going home, that he didn't have to sit here with trash excuses for Marines like Loya when he could be home getting drunk, and where was his respect as an officer, blah-blah-blah.

I would sneak Loya off the base after his last check-in so he didn't get completely consumed by the ordeal. One night we went to Greenville with the intent to pick up some college girls, but they smelled the stench of degradation on us from a mile away. We danced our asses off all night and approached just about every one of them with no success, and at the end of the night, while we were walking to our car, a girl yelled, "Go back to Lejeune, motherfuckers!" and started cackling like it was the funniest thing in the world.

"Hey, we just, like, came back from Afghanistan, you know," we blubbered.

In the end, the same barracks lawyers who had tried to give Loya advice while he awaited his punishment were the same ones who found him guilty in a matter of minutes during his court-martial. Loya didn't hold it against them; there wasn't anything they could really do. The Marine Corps had a "zero-tolerance" policy on drugs, and we had been kidding ourselves to think the poppy field defense would hold up. He compounded the problem by hiring a civilian lawyer, paid out of pocket by his parents, who believed that their son had been the victim of some kind of military scam involving faulty urinalysis kits. Loya was unceremoniously stripped of his rank, college benefits, and VA health care before he returned back home to El Paso. But at least he was a free man, and that's better than what I had going. I still had a year left on my contract.

————

The CNN video I made was honored at DINFOS with a military videography award, and afterward they gave the honorees vouchers to attend the White House News Photographers Association banquet. They had an open bar and the old wives of politicians kept bringing me drinks and asking if the Purple Heart hanging from my uniform was real. I got browned out and entered another version of myself, like a slick sea creature coming up for air, and began offending people during the ceremony. Soon the wives were whispering to me, "Honey, you should slow down," and there were sad glances being cast in my direction. The poor, wounded combat vet who was having trouble adjusting.

After the ceremony I got into a tiff with a bunch of Combat Camera Air Force officers who kept saying it was harder to take a great photo in your own backyard than it was in a combat zone—a direct jab at me, I knew—and I thought it would be funny if I gave one of them a little slap. But then his wife got in my face and I kind of smushed her away from me, drawing the whole lot of them on me until I was on the floor laughing hysterically because I knew if they just let me go I would show them how violent I could really be.

The bouncers threw me out—big guys who were probably ex–Secret Service—and I roamed the streets of DC until I invited myself into a Georgetown frat party. They were all shocked to see me and kept asking if I was really a Marine as I chased shots of Jägermeister with bong hits. I was half-aware of someone filming me the whole time, but it didn't bother me none; I was playing the character I was always destined to play.

I left a nondescript dorm room early enough the next morning to avoid the two girls I never did get straight enough to do much with. At some point I got a call from Chief Warrant Officer Walsh asking me what the hell happened last night. I had come up on a blotter, some kind of system that tracked incidents involving Marines, quote "in the commandant's own backyard," referring to the audacity I'd had to make a scene in DC, where the commandant of the Marine Corps lived.

Walsh asked me if I had PTSD, and I decided that the amount of shit I was in made it best to say "yeah." They demoted me and shaved my head and flew me back to town the next week to apologize to everyone at the banquet that I offended, half of whom I couldn't even remember.

A few incidents later and I was in the hospital, back with the red-lipped group counselor who tried to convince me to stay longer, which I did. It turned out to be the right move, because it prolonged the paperwork the military had to go through to have me administratively separated with an other-than-honorable discharge. After all, I wasn't there to sign anything. In appreciation of the counselor's generosity, I became de facto leader of her group meetings, and even chastised the others for thinking they were ready to leave when they hadn't done the work yet.

"I just feel like you've been wasting our time," I said to one of them on the last day of his stay in the hospital. "You haven't internalized anything. You haven't talked. You haven't even admitted to yourself that you have a problem. I see you drinking again as soon as you leave here. I'm just being honest." The poor guy looked like he was going to cry.

In the evenings, when they let us play volleyball, I would dominate mercilessly, jumping up and spiking the ball every chance I got, jumping and spiking and slamming the ball down with the force and conviction of a truly reformed individual.

"Give me respect, and keep me safe," the posters that lined the walls of the psych ward said, with pictures of patients smiling graciously. *Keep me safe*, I thought. I guess that was all we could hope for anymore.

CHAPTER 13

Scratching for a Niche

That was the way a lot of us said good-bye to each other, good-bye to the Marine Corps. After everything we'd been through together, we eked our way out with what little dignity we could maintain, left with a final shrug of farewell, splintering off into obscurity, no longer tethered together by the brotherhood the military had foisted upon us. Perhaps as a way to avoid moving on, I began working on the footage vociferously, and sort of desperately. I enrolled in Columbia University's film and media studies program, where I bored and weirded out my fellow students by showing endless cuts of bloody Bernhard being carried, then set down, then carried again, before the helicopter finally took him away.

I was trying to go against Hollywood, you see. They didn't want to show this kind of stuff in Hollywood. But it was oh-so-obvious and bewildering to them at the same time, my obsession with this stuff, and at some point I realized no one really cared. Not even me anymore.

I started having dreams about a mismanaged operation that no one can remember, but that I distinctly recall. Loya and I called it Gandy's Crusade, because it was led by Lieutenant Gandy of CNN video fame. Shortly after the mortar and grenade attack, they had gone out and done a blitzkrieg through the villages surrounding their patrol base, and, for some reason, they insisted on bringing Loya and me; I guess so we could document all the people they rounded up. We took over a house near the cliffs they'd been shooting at, and promptly, and pretty savagely, began detaining every military-aged male they could find. I remember the house because it was idyllic and we felt like we were living in *The Lord of the Rings* up there on the peak of the cliffs.

At night, the moon illuminated everything—you didn't need NVGs—and in the main room you could hear the stirring of the detained men, soft and quiet, as if they were trying to get comfortable without making too much noise. There was a shady counter-intelligence officer with an even shadier translator and a little book of Pashto phrases he kept in his chest pocket. He would take the men one by one into another room in the compound and question them, and each morning the children of the detainees would come to the compound asking when their fathers would be released. I never knew what the purpose of this exercise was; I guess they saw it as a way of throwing a wrench into the Taliban's plans, catching everyone off guard, but mostly it just confused and pissed off the locals, all of whom had work to do and lives to live that we were upending.

But in the dream, it's us who are detained in the compound, Loya and me. Except, no one is really watching us—it's more of a feeling that we're stuck there. There's an Afghan at one of the doors, but when we get up to leave, he just points out to the moon. There seems to be somewhere we're trying to get to, and we even rejoice a little once we get down off the cliff, but after we reach a certain

187

point, we end up back in the same mud hut with the same Afghan standing at the door. And now there are more Marines in the room with us, and they're scared and angry; their faces tell me everything. Every time we leave, the room gets more crowded when we return, until it's filling up to the point that there's no space to move, and our faces are only inches apart.

That's when I realize we're all dead, and this is where we go when we die, and if we try to stray too far, we'll just end up back here.

This dream actually became more real to me than the footage, because I had too much control over the footage, rewinding and cutting and juxtaposing it all. You begin to feel like you have the power to change the outcome. A firefight starts and stops because I hit the play button. Bernhard gets shot at 3 minutes and 13 seconds. We get blown up at 1 hour, 35 minutes, and 11 seconds. It's all mapped out. But I had no control with the dream. And that's how the unreality became more true to life.

Everything starts to feel like a video game after a certain point, anyway. You can't tell how much of what's in your head is you and how much is influenced by new media. What can be said that hasn't already been vlogged? What can be thought that doesn't come tinged with past thoughts? What can be filmed (or dreamed, for that matter) that can't be digitally reconstructed?

I read that they've started using video games as a way to treat PTSD. Soldiers and veterans describe their experience to a game designer, and they re-create the moments in the virtual world. The soldiers play the game as a way to get some exposure therapy. It's funny that the same tool that helped get us into the war is now being used to help us cope with coming back. Soon I think we'll have it perfected, this messy business of going and coming back.

"When I think back, my first thought is, like, what were the rules of engagement? Like, the *actual* ROEs," he said, taking a sip of beer. These days he was looking older and skinnier. I had convinced him to come stay with me in New York for a bit; he didn't have any money or plans so he agreed. Our movie didn't turn out the way we had hoped; there were no shrooms or suits, but I still needed Loya to feel like part of this was his just as much as it was mine.

Now, drinking with him in the shitty dive bar we were in, the residuals of what the Marine Corps had done to him could be seen etched into his face. The lightness in him was gone and replaced with an unfamiliar edge. In most cases, anyway, that lightness that once carried us, lifting us from doubt and allowing us to float, was also what made us killers. And time would not allow us to be killers forever; it was a young man's game. Questions needed answers, things that had gotten glossed over so swiftly and with such ease that it made your head spin when you stopped to look back.

"The first week, while you were with the snipers, I was with Weapons Company," he said, and took another drink.

"We would just walk down to the Helmand River and the DM would take shots at people from across it. They'd call it in and say, 'This guy's acting shady,' or 'We think we see a muzzle,' but it could just be a sickle. And it would always get approved. Afterwards there wouldn't be a BDA or anything, we wouldn't inspect the body, so we wouldn't know who we killed, good or bad. It was the same idea as Marjah, you know? Roll in there and fuck shit up, then transition to hearts and minds."

He even sounded different. The way he told war stories had changed—more weight, but the intonation wasn't the same, either.

Loya was one of the few Combat Camera guys who had actually killed someone on a deployment, which was something I didn't learn until after we'd gotten out (he was never much for bragging, as most guys would have). One day, the platoon he was with in Marjah was walking through a new AO when a guy stumbled out of a poppy field with an RPG, looking lost. Loya was the first to spot him and stared at the guy for a second before raising his rifle and putting a bullet in his face. He said the last thing he saw was the guy opening his mouth, as if there was something he wanted to say.

"It was weirder filming dudes kill people," he said, after we'd taken a shot of well whiskey that almost made me heave. Once you're a vet, you tend to perpetuate the same tropes as vets from past wars, seeking out the dingiest bars to get drunk in and reminisce about the old, dark times with nostalgia and awe. " 'Cause you're even more detached from what's happening," he went on, "in the sense that you're focused on getting the shot and nothing else, like you're not really there or something. We were also kinda hoping they'd do it, too, you know, for your movie and all."

The last one stung a bit, whether he'd meant it to or not; I'd always thought it was *our* movie even though we'd never gotten a chance to film the second half. If it was both of ours, it meant that there was an even share of guilt. I'd been working on it alone while in college, which was another ridiculous thing about what happened to Loya; he wasn't able to use the GI Bill because of his discharge. SEALs like Eddie Gallagher, who, while ultimately acquitted, was accused by his own platoon members of killing women and children for sport in Iraq got pardoned with full honors by Trump, while a low-level guy like Loya was left with a discharge status that followed him the rest of his life because he smoked pot in Afghanistan.

The old gullibility in him was gone, too. He no longer approached life with the openness and acceptance that once drew people to him. We were trying to work on the footage together, it was our new mission, but it was hard now. We'd lost the momentum we'd had when we were still Marines. The celebration of chaos and war less endearing now, without the framework of a killing machine around us. Now that I was in college, I realized that there needed to be more reflection in the film, a sense that what we'd taken part in was bad. I took an "anthropology of war" class at Barnard, Columbia's sister school, and I swear I could hear some of them hiss when I raised my hand to put in my two cents about Afghanistan. They were all socially awkward scaredy-cats—they didn't have the nerve to look you in the eye when they cast you as the villain—but goddamn if they weren't direct, if not outright correct, in explaining that we veterans were the bad guys. They were right, at least from a macro view.

It's crazy, but for a short time after I got out, I was able to convince myself that the truly fatalistic detractors of the war were missing something. A piece of the puzzle they would never understand because they didn't realize that we had made friends over there. Wahid, for example, the jaded Afghan terp who wouldn't stop flicking me in the head after I'd gotten hit with shrapnel, had made it to the States by schmoozing a colonel at the Kajaki Dam. He'd realized that getting shot at alongside us lance corporals in the killing fields was not going to get him a visa to America, so he became the personal translator for this colonel instead, who finally pushed his paperwork through.

Loya and I went to visit Wahid in Maryland to make sure he was adjusting okay. He was working as a bellhop at a Holiday Inn, and we would sneak him off the front desk to go get high in the vacant rooms and reminisce like we were back in Afghanistan. We were maintaining the illusion that we were all okay—psychologically, but also morally. We couldn't be war criminals if we had made friends with the locals, right? It's kind of like a White guy who says he can't be racist because he has Black friends.

The reality set in when, on one of our visits, we caught Wahid just as he'd been fired for being disrespectful to one of the hotel's guests.

"This guy comes down and says there is no towels in the room, and I say okay, here is some towels," he told us. "But then he just keep saying it, about the towels, and I told him okay, hold on, sir, I'll be right back." He stopped and waited for us to catch up to the punch line. "And then I just left."

The service industry in Afghanistan was a little different from here, and we could tell Wahid was fed up with American entitlement, something we hadn't forewarned him about when we were waxing lyrical for him all those nights at the dam. We'd smoke hookah and watch live performances of Alizée, the French Britney Spears he was obsessed with, off his hard drive, then tell him about all the things he had to look forward to when he got to the States. He was already there with us in his mind. Wahid had been almost fully Americanized by U.S. forces before he'd gotten to America. Through a toxic mix of exaggeration and hyperbole, fueled by the sexual boasting of Marines and sailors past, he had become one of us; a regular fuckboy in the making. "They will sleep with you the first time you meet them?" he'd ask. "Oh, yes," we'd say. The food, the drugs. You wouldn't believe it. You're gonna love it. We'd get off on telling him about it, just as he'd get off on hearing about it. That's what got him through nine different units' worth of combat operations, a total of six consecutive years in the war.

"I miss Afghanistan," he told us, now that he'd been in the U.S. for all of a year. We decided to show him cuts of the movie we were working on for nostalgia purposes, which was good fun until he spotted Seven, a translator we all knew. In the cut, I was interview-ing a Marine about something or other, when he came waltzing into the shot and sat down next to him, oblivious to what we were doing.

"Get the fuck out of my shot," you can hear me saying in the video.

"No, it's okay," Seven says, with a nonchalant flick of the wrist.

Wahid suddenly paused the video.

"He's dead," he said.

"Who?" we asked.

"Husan. Well, Seven, I think you called him, his call sign or whatever. They beheaded him."

We all sat there in silence for a moment. Seven, now Husan, as we were just now learning, was one of the coolest terps we knew. He was always making 550-cord bracelets for people, and singing or cracking jokes. There was a devil-may-care vibe to him and I now wondered, in that defensive part of the brain that forces you to find something to blame for all things tragic, if it was at least partly responsible for his death. One time, after I'd received a bottle of whiskey disguised in a Listerine bottle from a friend back home, we'd gotten drunk together at the FOB, and Husan had gone com-pletely off the rails, running into the sergeant major and battalion commander's tent to call them infidels. We had to abandon him at that point, lest we all got into trouble.

"You're not even that drunk," we had told him. He'd only had a couple of swigs, but he didn't care; he was having a good time getting it off his chest.

"Fuck," Loya and I said.

"Yeah," said Wahid. "He was a really good guy." Why should we be the ones who got to go home scot-free, when people like Husan were left to get their heads cut off? "America shouldn't have gotten involved in Afghanistan," Wahid said. "I used to think you were going to help us, but now I see it was all bullshit. Also, your movie sucks."

"It's still a work in progress," we told him.

He showed us the Adam Curtis documentary *Bitter Lake* on YouTube. If you've never seen it, it's a film that manages to capture the history and feeling of Afghanistan with music and stock footage in such a way that it becomes a part of you forever. Wahid and I still listen to the soundtrack anytime we see each other. And he was right, *Bitter Lake* made us realize that yes, our movie did suck.

———

Things with Loya started devolving shortly thereafter. I had just gotten married and my wife, Ciara, and I were living in a one-bedroom in Midwood, Brooklyn, Loya crashed out on the couch. He was supposed to be looking for a job while we worked on the movie, but he was clearly dead inside. It was like he could only summon half a try at anything, too afraid to go beyond that because whatever it was, he knew it would soon fall apart, like what had happened in the Marines. I tried to ignore his negativity because to make art you have to fool yourself into thinking that what you're making is important, and has something to it that people are going to give a shit about. So, we'd get high and brainstorm, but mostly we just reminisced about the funny times and the bad times, while Ciara grew increasingly annoyed with our regressive behavior.

Things ended for good one day when, after we all went to take acid in the Catskills with my wife and her friends, Loya freaked out and thought we had tricked him into taking it alone. "I don't feel safe," he kept saying, scanning the tree lines and looking suspiciously at a waterfall we had all posted up under. "Something's not right."

I tried to convince him it was all good, that we were all tripping, but he didn't believe me, and it didn't help that my wife and her friends giggled at us hysterically the whole time while I crouched down and tried to whisper him back down to earth. A bad omen had been planted inside him, and he wasn't going to let it get away until it had shown him everything it had to offer. That was the way with Loya—he took omens and dreams and such very seriously.

He went back to El Paso a couple of weeks later, ignoring my pleas for him to stay so we could finish the movie. I felt myself getting sick because I didn't have the balls to be real with him and tell him that he was my best friend, that I didn't want him to leave because he was my only connection to the past, and that I was scared of what was going to happen to him. He got into a car accident right after he got back to El Paso, a crash he'd later claim was intentional. He had been drinking and listening to Bob Seger all day when he pulled into his parents' cul-de-sac and sat there with the car idling for a few minutes, before revving it up and flying down the street to crash into a telephone pole. He then got out of his car and into his parents' car and got back on the freeway.

He went missing until his friend Pablo was finally able to flag him down and get him off the road. Loya told me he might have been trying to kill himself but wasn't sure. He had lost his faith, and as a man of God that was a big deal for him. He was left to rely on his own internal source of spirituality, a source he'd later say was actually the devil in disguise.

Trying to right the wrongs that Loya and I had made—the half-hearted attempts at a "hybrid doc" that combined fiction and nonfiction, the overuse of music to make up for lack of story or thematic structure—Ciara and I set out to make a straightforward documentary, in the conventional sense, with plans to record new interviews with the guys from the footage, now able to speak with time and distance to reflect. It was 2016, three years after I'd returned home.

We drove all across the country, and Ciara, who is from Ireland, saw the America we were trying to forget existed—the big, empty sprawl that was home to half of the country. There was a common thread among the guys I talked to. Most were willing to say the war had been a shit show, doomed from the start, a failure on the part of the politicians and generals who'd sent us out there—a crime even—but no one was really willing to blame ourselves for the war's outcome.

"We did the best we could, given the fucked-up situation," Tony said. Crazy Tony, the roided-out freak whose main aspiration during our deployment had been to terrorize the local children in as many creative ways as he could imagine, who used to chase them around with his Glock and toss them into wadis, was now, I shit you not, training to become a psychiatrist. "I wanna help other guys who are going through the same shit you and I went through," he told me, flashing a grin that showed off a set of newly restored veneers. Gone was the hillbilly gap in his incisors that had made him even more menacing; he now had a completely new set of teeth courtesy of the U.S. Department of Veterans Affairs. He was also collecting 100 percent disability for PTSD, which worked out to a monthly stipend of more than $3,000 a month.

"It's back pay, the way I see it. Because we didn't get paid shit while we were out there." We were watching him inhale a family-size platter of forty hot wings at a Buffalo Wild Wings in Virginia, my wife and I in a state of awe, half-unbelieving that he was going to finish them all by himself. His wife said he definitely was. He was even bigger now than when I knew him in Afghanistan. He had been in a few bodybuilding competitions since then, and he liked to post pictures of himself in an American flag Speedo at the gym to Instagram, alongside other pictures of him and the rest of the Four Locos from Afghanistan: standing in a pot field, holding a pistol to his head in mock suicide. He looked like a giant, crazy, bulging hot dog with sun-white teeth, and a ventriloquist dummy beard that looked drawn on.

The clackity chatter in his teeth when he spoke made me question what speedy supplements he might be on, but I could tell he was happy now. His wife was expecting a kid soon, and he had learned to channel all his stress and anger into the gym. The other Four Locos from his platoon (Rodriguez, Valdez, and Klasko) had all lost touch with each other, and though this distance made Tony sad, he knew he was doing all right nonetheless. Besides, he said, "Rodriguez's a fat piece of shit now. Have you seen the photos of him and his wife?" He pulled them up on his phone to show me, shaking his head disgracefully. This was a criminal offense to Tony, getting out of shape.

I don't know what I was expecting, going around talking to these guys. I think I was hoping to see change and growth. I wanted to film them watching the old versions of themselves and see a sense of shame and embarrassment at their younger, less thoughtful, sadistic selves. Some sign that they had matured into responsible human beings since then. I wanted justification for loving them, because I had loved them at one point, had called them good friends. I would have gone out on a limb to help them, and I still felt a thrill at seeing them again, like something lost was being reconnected. I was, of course, hoping for my own absolution for filming them in their dreadful acts, too.

But in this new context, outside the war, I realized they were mostly unlikable dipshits. Or maybe that was precisely what had made them likable in the first place, because to be functional in a war zone you have to be at least partly a dipshit. Regardless, many of them had doubled down on their Marine personas. It was as if they wanted to hold on to what the Corps had made them, because to let go of it was to be nothing again, and it was too late in the game to start from scratch. We were already at high risk.

My main hope in interviewing Tony, and the thing I was most nervous about because I wasn't sure how he'd react (confusion, distrust, even potential hostility), was to see him make amends for the things he'd done to the kids. If he was studying to become a shrink, he surely must appreciate the trauma he had imprinted on those young Afghan boys and girls who weren't old enough at the time to comprehend what he was doing to them, and didn't speak the language in order to discern his actions.

I sat him down and pulled out my laptop, while Ciara, who was fascinated by Tony's nature ("He's *so* American," she kept saying), filmed him. The video started and there was Afghan Tony in his natural habitat; younger, sleeker, the video so overplayed in my mind that it seemed to propel him to action, as if he was pushed to move by some crazy future documentary strings, grabbing the pistol from his holster and pointing it with two hands (this making it even more audacious) at some kids approaching on their donkeys. Screaming at them and shoving the gun in their faces. In my arrogance, I imagined Tony's face as these images flashed in front of him for the first time in years: a mask of estrangement, shame, resignation. This was evidence of how we became creatures of ourselves to make it through, a depiction of how we coped with our fear.

But as soon as the video started, Tony was doubled over laughing, barely able to contain himself, the dip spit bottle in his hand almost spilling on my computer. It was a struggle for him just to keep watching with each new convulsion. I wanted to cut it right there, to tell Ciara to stop recording, because this was not helping the cause. This would only make Tony more Tony.

"Oh my gawwwd," his wife moaned, watching the video. It was her first time seeing this, which was also a concern for me; after all, this was going to be the father of her kids. But she seemed okay with it. I watched Tony, still in stitches, and wondered if there was a performative layer to his overly raucous laughter that was brought on by my filming him, once again. Is this what he thought I wanted? That I was just there to help the boys relive the glory days?

"I said get off the donkey, bitch," Afghan Tony said in the video, grabbing a kid with one hand and jabbing the gun at him with the other. The kid was shielding himself with his arm.

"Get off the donkey, bitch," Tony echoed in real time, as if re-learning the lines to one of his favorite forgotten songs.

"He's gonna cry," Rodriguez said, laughing behind the camera, the soulless ghost of scumbag cinematographers.

"Where's the fucking Taliban?" Tony was almost whispering now to one of the children he held at gunpoint.

Tony was the bad-apple ambassador we all hated but secretly admired. Marines, by nature, are supposed to be bad apples—we were Uncle Sam's Misguided Children (USMC)—and he had the moxie to embody it to its full extent; he was the reddest, juiciest, most sickening apple you could stomach. At the end, video Tony, a smirk on his face, pulled out a piece of chocolate for the kids, who were now realizing that this was how Americans joked. Some of them cracked hesitant smiles, while others continued to keep their distance. Some of them laughed. The kid took the chocolate. Rodriguez dropped the camera. The video ended.

"Ahhh," Tony exhaled, wiping a tear from his eye. "What else ya got?"

I saw that the Marine Corps had only exacerbated Tony's condition. He was something vile before he was a Marine, and now he was living on a thin wire, an amalgamation of Ritalin and American bullyism turned inward and coagulated into something thirsty and reckless. He was still a shark who saw the children with the same dehumanizing gaze as when we were enlisted, and the fun and games we played were still just that to him, fun and games; what bored Marines did in a combat zone. I also realized that I was the same coward and freak like him, because a secret part of me still found the video funny. And I wasn't going to reprimand Tony, the same way I hadn't stopped him from pelting that old man with rocks.

Ciara never quite looked at me the same after that. To her, it was a grown man in uniform, a symbol of both imperialism and mental decay, threatening and scaring the living shit out of some innocent kids in a third-world country. I said no, it was a kid playing with some other kids in a war zone.

———

Next we were off to find Lance Corporal Schmuckatelli himself (his real name was actually pretty close to Schmuckatelli). I'd heard he was in upstate New York, near Cooperstown. If Tony hadn't changed, then maybe Schmuckatelli had. After popping on the urinalysis, like Loya, he'd gotten the boot with an other-than-honorable discharge and was left without money for college or VA health care. He was working a landscaping job and I'd heard he was struggling after his wife had left him. He'd been in and out of rehab, etc. Surely he would be a new man, a sane and sympathetic man to offset the guys like Tony; or at the least he could be a charity case. And I was right. The fuck-you scowl was gone from his face and had been replaced with an opioid glaze; oxycodone eyes and Xanax lips that were sort of filmy, like sad-boy silicon. I showed him the interview I'd conducted with him all those years ago, where he said he wished everyone in Afghanistan would die, how gay everyone was and how much he hated their guts, and he sat there watching, squinting his eyes in consternation.

"Yeah, I don't think that way anymore," he said. "It's hard to watch." He seemed to be in a state of constant doubt about who he was now, more soft-spoken. We went out to film him petting a horse his wife had left in their backyard. She'd taken off after he'd gone out back one night to fire his shotgun at nothing, a way to "relieve stress" after an argument. His wife had called Schmuckatelli's brother for advice on the matter and he called the cops. A SWAT team showed up in full tactical gear and he surrendered obligingly, so drunk that he wasn't really sure what was happening.

"I was a fuckup before I got in the Marines," he told me. "That's who they attract. The Corps is basically just a gang, like the Bloods or the Crips." He looked around the room as his eyes fell on his Purple Heart, still encased in its box, sitting on his wife's dresser. A reward for getting shot in the arm on one of his deployments.

I asked him if he ever got that motorcycle he'd been longing for. He took me to his car and showed me the court-ordered Breathalyzer he had been sentenced to blow into to start it. He'd had three DUIs since getting out of the Marines, so maybe a motorcycle was a bad idea. "Or maybe better, since I'd only be putting myself at risk," he said, a concerning lilt to his voice. Even though he was in rehabilitation, we still went to a bar—my idea, because being around him was making me want to drink, and I wasn't going to curtail my substance abuse on his behalf. I ordered a beer and he ordered a rum and Coke, taking it sip by sip self-consciously like he was expecting it to jump up and bite him. It was after the third or fourth round that we ran out of things to talk about, memories to relive, and he started talking politics.

"Obama came out here," he said. "Everyone lost their shit. I was like, really? You're excited to see *that* nigger?"

I looked across the bar at the other midday drinkers and felt a hole in my chest that would never be filled. "Thank you for your time," I said as we parted. "Lance Corporal Schmuckatelli."

CHAPTER 14

Freedom in Bliss

The country was collapsing spiritually and mentally around us, around me. It was part of the *Avatar* effect; things were so stale and fake that men were hoarding guns in an unabashed attempt to solidify themselves as men. They'd leap past metaphor into open idiocy. You take away our masculinity, our sense of reality, and we will become the caricatures you all despise, they were saying. We'll wear 5.11 Tactical hats and get meaningless sleeve tattoos and create Instagram accounts where we get other men riled up, too. We'll playact *Fight Club* and go mental deconstructing UFC bouts, analyzing blows we'd never think to throw ourselves. And we'll wear that fucking camo *everywhere*.

I first noticed the camo fetish in my periphery after I had enlisted in 2008; large, shapeless men with goatees and buzz cuts at the airport sporting the same camouflage jackets and backpacks we'd worn in the field. At first I thought, *Okay, I guess they support the troops*. But then it morphed into something else. Now, in America, people go to weddings in camo, they have family dinners in camo, they give birth in camo. Men have gotten jobs because they're wearing camo, and women have formed bonds with other women over their shared appreciation of camouflaged garments. I realized they were trying to look like us, not as a sign of support for what we'd fought for, but in support of *fighting* in general. The lumberjack look that a lot of the vets I knew at Columbia embodied—the plaid shirt and desert-camouflaged American flag hat—the bearded "operator" look, was now a symbol of *the resistance*, whatever that meant.

It wasn't even funny anymore. They killed the joke when they fully embodied the satire. And here I was still trying to make a movie out of the war. I knew I had sent this shit into hyperdrive. In my own contrived way, I was trying to absolve us, but the guys I'd sweated and bled alongside wouldn't let me. In their eyes, they didn't need absolving. They were becoming a part of something bigger than themselves again.

———

"Fuck Hillary Clinton," Platt said when I asked him if he had anything else he wanted to add at the end of our interview. He said it, then raised his eyebrows at me as if to make sure I'd fully registered the weight of this statement. We'd been out all day waiting to shoot a coyote. Platt still wanted me to film him in action—this was the second act of his movie, after all—and so we had set out into the woods near his parents' house with him riding on the back of a four-wheeler operated by a friend of his, a silent young man who seemed to be some kind of personal lackey to Platt, and more than once he'd rolled off the thing and we had to set him back in. It was hard to strap him in without his legs, and so he just held on tight for the short ride into a clearing where he told me the wolves liked to roam.

I felt sick from the McDonald's breakfast sandwich I'd gotten that morning in Munford, Tennessee. They'd lathered the thing with a yellow substance I wasn't sure was mayonnaise or cheese, or both, and all I knew was that I'd never seen anything like it before and it made me feel terrible. In hindsight, the outcome of the upcoming presidential election should have been apparent to me then and there. That radioactive gooey substance being dealt out by the barrelful in Anytown, USA, and the fact that everything else in Platt's town was boarded up except for the Jack in the Box and Taco Bell. The area had developed a taste for meta-fakeness; to "be real" in southern terms meant being able to embrace being full of shit.

When I first greeted Platt, I put my hand on his shoulder while he wheeled up next to me, and he glared at it sharply until I removed it. I realized people were probably always trying to touch him, out of pity or attempted support, or even just fetishistic curiosity.

"You shoulda been there recording when I stepped on that IED," he said, reprimanding me. "I went up like a *rocket*." He said "rocket" like he was ready to take off again. He was a massive ball of love and sadness and fury, and humor. There was something old-lady-like in his attitude to everything, like an old southern belle who's been-there-done-that and doesn't have time for the constant frivolities. He laughed at the irony of the fact that he liked to shoot home-made fertilizer bombs in his backyard, the same kind the Taliban had blown his legs off with.

"Guess it's therapeutic, or somethin'," he told me, watching the smoke drift off of one that he'd just shot with a modded-out M4 rifle.

Rosales and Boone had been out to visit him a few times, but everyone else from his platoon had 86'd him. Each year Bernhard's mom held a reunion for all the guys at her house on the day he died, and at one of the reunions some kind of epic drama had occurred that no one would fully explain to me. Now Platt wasn't welcome anymore. It made sense—you get a bunch of combat vets together and feed them beer and have them relive certain things, and there's going to be some stuff that comes up—but it also seemed massively petty. Here Platt was, legless up to the hips, and they couldn't forgive him for wanting to play the game, same as them, only a little harder.

When I asked Elmira what that was about, he said he wasn't sure, but that some of the things he'd done just didn't sit well with the rest of the squad. After we returned to the States, Platt had gotten written up for a Silver Star, and in the write-up Platt had said he carried Bernhard the whole time, just like when I'd interviewed him. He had also appeared in a segment on Headline News where he added a part about carrying Bernhard up a cliff while getting shot at.

I said, "Sure, he's mythologizing the experience; it probably helps him cope with everything."

"Okay, that's all fine and dandy, but why's it always gotta be about him?" Elmira replied. "Like, okay, Platt, you lost your legs, but every guy who loses their legs don't go on *Duck Dynasty*, or get sponsored by the Gary Sinise Foundation, or get a house built for them by Home Depot." It was true; Platt had been touted as some kind of golden disabled vet by the media and various charity organizations. He had made headlines when he wept openly on an airliner that refused to give him a better seat, and I think he'd even made it to the stage at a Trump rally or two. All that attention was not deserved, the others thought, especially Bernhard's mom.

But maybe Platt was just a man of the times. He was the reality TV killer; he embodied the knowledge that our moments of living aren't really substantial anymore, that they don't matter unless they're captured on camera. He didn't go on a hunting trip without a camera crew and five GoPros strapped to his head and rifle. In that Trump-like way, he would have a hard time existing if he couldn't post his thoughts and actions onto social media, because what else are you living for? This change came on fast in the years our cohort got out of the military, and it rattled a lot of vets, myself included. The new social media landscape felt like a gutted, stripped-down version of the lifestyle we'd had in the service. We had lived on top of each other, anonymous to the outside, but deeply connected to each other. Now we saw guys living life *only* for the outside, defining what "the Marines" meant for the world, with no care for what their fellow vets thought about.

The coyote never came, so Platt and I just shot targets and then he wheeled around his parents' house talking about the new house that was getting built for him that would be fully handicapped accessible and operable. I showed him the raw footage of Bernhard getting shot, which made him tear up years after he had last seen it. I tried to cry, too, but I couldn't.

I left with some good shots of Platt saying, "I'd ride that wave again, brother. If I had the chance, hell yeah, I'd ride that wave again. Because that was my identity, that was who I was. You know me, man. I was gonna be a lifer...." And his voice caught, and I wondered, even though he was on camera, if it was the first time Platt was being real with me, or if there was a distinction between his on- and off-camera personas anymore.

When I got home afterward, I pulled my old cammies out of the closet, the same ones that Bernhard's blood had spilled onto while we were trying to medevac him. Shortly before I joined, the uniform design changed from the traditional Vietnam-era brush-stroke camouflage to digital camo. "Digies," we called them, because they appear pixelated, making us look like we'd been rendered in low resolution. It's a fitting look for the internet-era soldier, but jarringly so. It made me feel like a simulation. If I died my death might go unregistered, or worse, another me would respawn somewhere else.

The splotch of Bernhard's blood was no longer red, but a faded brown that seemed to mix in with the desert color of the digital camouflage. The real mixing with the artificial.

When I finished a rough cut of the movie, I sent it to the Pentagon so they could review it for classified material, even though I knew none of it was. For something to be classified, it has to reveal top-secret information, like unreleased weapons systems, or compromising information about secret informants, or places that we weren't supposed to be. It's pretty hard for the Pentagon or DoD to classify stuff just because it makes them look bad, especially when it's your garden-variety footage of lance coolies smoking hash in the field during America's longest war. Or dead civilians. But I wanted to cover my ass, in case the Marine Corps tried to say that it wasn't properly reviewed before I sent it out to film festivals.

Nonetheless, the cut of what I'd been working on must have scared the shit out of them. I had enlisted the help of a grad student at Columbia named Eric Schuman. Schuman was a godsend, but he was also a bit of a wild card, a neurotic, twenty-five-year-old recluse who ate, drank, and slept film editing. He was capable of anything if you gave him enough time, but you also had to give him restraints. He took a look at the interviews I'd done with the guys after traveling around the country for a year and said we should scrap them all. Instead he wanted a stream of montages cut together using only the Afghan footage—a meta-montage. I almost wanted to kill him at first. What was he trying to say by stripping everything of its context? Now, in his version, the clip of Tony chasing the kids was spliced with other clips, as if it were no different from the rest of the war. During the firefight when we were shooting at the cliffs, he'd found a clip of a guy saying we should just start bombing everyone in the nearby village and they'd "get the idea." He found a shot that Loya had gotten at some point of Marines handing out cigarettes to some toddlers, and when the kids started lighting up and smoking, you can hear someone in the background cackling, "Fuckin' dune niggers." Clearly Schuman lacked the nuance required for this type of material. He wanted to paint us as monsters.

But then I saw it was true. We did and said those things, and if anyone had a problem with it, then they had a problem with the war, and the military. And that was okay. Sometimes you have to scare the shit out of people to make them see the world for what it really is. No, the Marine Corps is not a bunch of patriotic go-get-'em kids who want to lay down their lives for their country. Yes, it is a fundamentally racist institution whose racist ire at the moment is directed at anyone who happens to be living in a Muslim country. No, boot camp does not build character; it trains you to turn your most sadistic tendencies up as high as they can go. Yes, we should know this by now. And no, the war in Afghanistan did not make sense, even if you used all the editing tricks in the book to make a movie out of it.

When you're working with combat footage, you instinctively try to guide the viewer, to make them understand what's happening. But half the time we didn't even understand what was happening. And the context was there in the messy and disordered cut of the film. That *was* the context for all the unnecessary death and destruction, for our fucked-up behavior and scumbag antics; it could be heard breathing behind the camera.

As much as I respect people like Sebastian Junger, documentaries like *Restrepo* still worked to make sense of the "mission." By coaxing an arc and clear directive out of the war, they gave people justification for what we were doing. Insane things that were evident on the ground, like the absurdity of a bunch of foreigners occupying the rural parts of a country they couldn't point out on a map, and acting as police for people who didn't understand what they were doing, became more sane after some storyboarding and edits. It's like the acronyms we used for everything: COIN, CAG, HUMINT, HUMRO—they didn't really mean anything or make sense half the time, but the more you repeated them the more legitimized they became. All you had to do was zoom out, and take a step back, to see that the underlying assumptions we make when we think about war and American occupation are flawed.

———

I thought I was going to have a panic attack at the first festival showing for *Combat Obscura*. All the years I spent working on it had lent me separation from the material, but there was nowhere for me to hide when it hit the big screen. The severity and irredeemableness of what we did in Afghanistan came down on me like a sledgehammer. I couldn't make eye contact during the Q&A, and I kept swaying back and forth staring at the floor. I must have looked like the perfect PTSD'd-out idiot up there. I regretted it all, and I almost cursed Schuman out because it was his idea to make the movie the way it was. There were no breaks in the car crash, no letup to allow the audience to breathe, I thought. Or maybe it was just me who hadn't inhaled.

After that first screening, I drank. Then I drank some more. I decided it was best this way. And because I no longer recognized my friends or myself in the film, I got bitter, and sad. I didn't want to explain the war for people. I didn't want the baggage, or the weird looks and responses, when they found out where I had been. I didn't want to be responsible for anyone's feelings getting hurt after watching the film. I didn't want to be a veteran. I never did.

I want to be judged, but not too harshly. I want you to call me a baby-killer, but not to my face. I want the veteran identity to be surgically extracted from my body, but I want you to buy me a beer so we can talk about the war, and the good times, and the bad times, and the rotten culture of the military, and the feeling of being young and in uniform and sexy and structured and free and a slave. I want you to get me to admit that I miss it.

Ciara was not impressed with my Q&A's where I'd get blackout drunk and start dropping f-bombs incessantly and not respecting the audience's questions, and making people feel uncomfortable. And we fought throughout the whole tour, because I was sick of it. At a festival in France, a young woman cursed me out because she said the movie was irresponsible. It could recruit the most vulnerable people (the Afghans) into joining the Taliban, and then they might end up vaporized by one of our drone strikes. I said that was the same fucking thing the government was saying about the film, just on the opposite end of the spectrum; they were concerned it could get *our* guys killed.

Ciara said I had been condescending to the Frenchwoman. She knew I was no different from the guys in the movie. That by recording them, I had made them do those things, to a degree. That I was an instigator and an unreliable narrator.

I said she could be a real thoughtless, heartless bitch.

"*You're* the bitch," she said. "*Oh, poor veteran. I'm so sorry you decided to go film people killing people and now you're sad and angry. Like, get over yourself.*" And we laughed because it was true. And then we fought because it was true.

"What about Bernhard?" I'd ask. "You don't care about Bernhard?"

"You didn't even know him that well!" she'd say, and I'd start crying like a bitch.

Who he was to me was the question I could never bear to answer, because it meant reevaluating who I was to him, to the rest of the guys, and to his mother, who would have to live with the fact that people were now paying to see her son die. In a way the videos were what kept me hopelessly stuck to the war, incapable of moving on until I'd pieced it all together just the right way, and then once that happened it could finally drift away. But of course it didn't. I just created a new war in my head; a war of ideas and tattered allegiances.

When I really wanted to stir things up, I would go into graphic detail to Ciara about the guy we executed, how if she only knew what a fucking monster I was, she'd leave me. But she wasn't buying it. If we were going to split up it would be because of *me* and *my* shit, *my* inability to move past it, not her judgment of the things I had done.

The vet community response after its online release was polarized, like everything else. Some saw it as a necessary insider's look into what the war was really like, while others thought it painted the military in an intentionally false and negative light. Others argued that, even if it was an accurate depiction of combat, civilians weren't up to the challenge of taking in that kind of heavy truth. The Marine Corps, however, was not as ambiguous in its response, and threatened to sue me for theft of government property. The brass was pissed about what I'd done, and I can't say I didn't understand why.

Luckily, the Knight First Amendment Institute at Columbia

University took up my case on First Amendment grounds. Before taking on *Combat Obscura*, they had litigated the release of information about the CIA's black sites and abuses at Guantanamo. They had sued Trump for blocking people on Twitter and had worked with people similar to Edward Snowden, so my issue was pretty small potatoes for them. In the end, the Marine Corps backed down from pursuing legal action, I think mostly because of the Knight Institute's backing, but also because they didn't want to give the film any more added publicity by dragging me into court.

———

One day a former sniper from the unit called me. He said the guys were pissed about me showing footage of a dead civilian they'd killed, especially without any context. They had maintained the belief over all the years that it was a good kill, even if it didn't look that way in the video. It didn't look that way at the time, either. From what I could remember of the incident, the snipers had justified it by saying the guy was "acting weird" and "running around barefoot." When we got to the body, and I started recording, they talked about hiding the corpse.

"They still think that guy was a bad guy?" I asked him. I was surprised. "I thought there was definitive evidence to the contrary."

"What the fuck are you talking about, dude?" he said. "What definitive evidence?"

"He was unarmed. Didn't even have a radio. And the locals said he was retarded."

"Okay. One local says he's retarded, another says he's in college. Everyone's got a different narrative. Who you gonna believe?"

I thought about this for a second. I told him I no longer knew what to believe, because any way you looked at it, we didn't really know what the fuck we were doing out there. "It wasn't our country," I said. "How could you be sure, I mean really sure, someone who wasn't armed was bad before taking the shot?"

He sighed heavily, as if to even ask meant I would never get it, and started to explain about how they would observe the people, how you could tell a dude was suspicious by the way other locals reacted to him, the patterns that the farmers exhibited and the "contrast of background." He described military-aged males moving in a "military manner," and how sometimes the Taliban would use women and children as shields when they carried their weapons. He talked about Icom chatter and other things, until I could tell he was getting pretty worked up.

"Look, you gotta understand, this is really personal shit," he said.

"Of course it is."

"Nobody wants their memory corrupted, and that's basically what you've done." We let it sit for a while, and I thought maybe he was going to hang up. "The truth is we shouldn't have ever fucking been there in the first place. If I was a local, I'd be shooting at us, too. But when . . . when you're out there you have to look at all the variables and outcomes and the worst-case scenario. What happens if you don't take the shot? Everything comes back to you or your friends getting killed. Would you rather be judged by twelve or carried by six?"

It was easy to think this way, sort of like saying "War is hell, so why be held accountable for anything?" But even though I hated (*hated*) who we were and what we'd been, I still couldn't help but feel the same respect for him that I'd always had for the guys. He was the man at one point, charged with doling out death before his brain was even fully developed enough to figure out who he was. And that was a tough thing to be left with, even if we were criminals.

"That whole experience doesn't deserve context," he said finally. "And that's why I'll always defend your documentary, because there shouldn't be any context for what happened out there, and what we did."

I still had questions, but he told me he had to go. "I don't want to talk about this with you anymore, man," he said, before hanging up the phone.

———

In 2019, I finally made it to one of Bernhard's memorial reunions in North Carolina. I figured I owed it to his mom to show my cowardly face, even though I knew some of the guys probably didn't trust me. Seeing them for the first time in six years made me wonder if I had ever really known them. A lot of them had swelled and developed shady, festering looks in their eyes that gave the impression they might have done some jail time at one point or another since getting out. When we were in the war, we were kids posturing as killers. Now we didn't have to posture anymore. We had killed, some of us, and the anger we were left with had congealed into something harder and more lethal, fed by adulthood outside the Corps, seasoned with life's disappointments and failures. As a rule, they weren't happy about the state of things. Freedoms were being taken away, they said, as they showed off arsenals of rifles stowed in the trunks of their cars, ready to be shown off in the parking lot outside the venue.

"No guns while y'all are drinking!" Susan, Bernhard's mom, yelled from the house.

"We know, Mom," they called back. They all called her "Mom," which was sweet and also kind of trashy at the same time. But she loved it, having all her boys home. It almost felt like her son was still alive.

"This is a place where they can come and let loose a little, and yeah, sometimes things get crazy, but they're safe here," she told me. She worked for a brewing company that made beer specifically for veterans and Gold Star families, and she handed me a can with a picture of Bernhard superimposed on it. It was a still from the death video I'd filmed—a shot of him on the roof moments before he got shot in the head. I didn't know how to feel about that.

"I'm just glad I was able to see the raw footage that you showed me," she said. "And finally see the truth about what happened that day."

I asked her what she meant by that.

"That Platt made up everything. He lied about it all."

I began to see that it wasn't so much the fact that Platt had lied about carrying Bernhard, and that the others were still carrying Bernhard in their hearts, but that he'd taken the spotlight away from her son. She and Platt had a lot in common; they were both trying to stay relevant in a world that was increasingly trying to forget about the sacrifices they made. She had a shrine in the living room for Bernhard, his boot camp photo at the front, mixed among school pictures and shots of him in Afghanistan from his first tour with a different battalion. She simply would not let him be forgotten. But the animosity she felt toward Platt was persistent in a way that I couldn't quite place. If she was the squad's mother now, Platt was an estranged father, or maybe more of an embittered grandmother.

"Did you see the post he made on Facebook? About 'Muslims go back to your country'?" she asked me. "I messaged him and said, 'Platt, you do realize that Sabbagh is a Muslim, right?' He goes, 'Oh, not ones like him.'" The chuckle that followed showed she wasn't as far gone as Platt had gotten, but a few minutes later, when the topic of the Taliban retaking control of Afghanistan came up, I heard her say we should just nuke the place. "They'll repopulate," she said confidently.

I wasn't sure if she knew about the wounded man we cornered and killed on Bernhard's behalf; I didn't know if that was something the others even still thought about. I certainly didn't have the gall to bring it up. I did wonder how she would feel about it, though; if she would be happy or not. My guess was yes, as some kind of minor conciliation that it hadn't all been for nothing; that we'd extracted revenge on the fucker who might or might not have gotten her son.

Elmira was a redneck hippy now. He had long hair and a beer gut with a seat belt scar running through it that he enjoyed showing off to everyone. He was taking acid in his RV, which was parked in the backyard of Susan's house, where she lived with her two other sons, her daughter-in-law, and her grandkid. Elmira had won the RV in some kind of veterans' raffle. He was much more aware of things now, he told me. I overheard him explaining to another hillbilly from his squad how the Afghans weren't "bad people by nature, they were just put into a shit situation, like us."

The hillbilly took a swig from his beer and swayed around a bit, said something unintelligible. "No," Elmira said. "No, because they were just trying to live their lives. Caught in the middle. What would you have done?" Then he gave me a wink.

"That's some pretty controversial shit you did," he said to me later in confidence inside his RV. "Lotta people are butt-hurt about it." He pulled out a hoodie that he'd printed a bunch of images onto. It looked like a snuff film collage. There were shots of the guys goofing around in Afghanistan and when they got back. A baby picture of Bernhard and Susan (looking very nineties hot mom) was next to a meme of a girl with her head shot off that said "Life hack: Use a curling iron to warm up a dead hooker's vagina." It was basically the internet printed on a sweatshirt, all too fitting. No one embodies the stark contrasts and brain-flipping idiosyncrasies of the internet more than Marines. Everything and nothing, all at once.

And there in the corner was a picture of the poster for *Combat Obscura*.

Doc Coleman was there, too, eying me suspiciously the whole time. "You're not recording this, are you?" he kept asking. He was still in the Navy, going on twelve years, and we were still his little lambs to keep safe.

"Jackson doesn't drink before five p.m.," he ordered.

"All right, Doc," they grumbled, and someone would go looking to make sure Jackson wasn't drinking yet. It was the cutest game ever played, the fact that they still took their roles to heart. Elmira was still a squad leader. Doc was still Doc. If we had started taking contact from the woods surrounding Susan's house, I'm sure they would have lined up in squad formation, grabbing the rifles out of their trunks and shouting out commands to each other. And I probably would have started filming. I had to admit, I felt that sense of wickedness and reckless abandon that day. The same way I used to *feel out there*, back before I had the compulsion to try to analyze where *that feeling* came from (or the constant urge to pull out the crutch in my pocket as a way to avoid looking at the world, or into people's eyes—by which I mean my smartphone, of course). Back when we knew that to question our instincts was to miss out on the truth of a certain code of doing, that to know it was to diminish it, the thing stemming from a primitive sense of who we were, or the idea we had of that primitive side of ourselves. That to question these "primitive" instincts of action and identity was really a form of complacency and longing for safety; the secret truth of Billy the Kid or whoever it was that said "It takes more guts to rob a bank than to run for president." A line of thinking we'd identified as toxic masculinity in the years that had passed.

"I miss the feeling in my balls," someone said. "The feeling of getting shot at. In your balls." He was staring at the bonfire burning in the backyard, eyes glazed over in full caveman mode. Because of course.

"He thinks he's one of us," Jackson drunkenly mumbled after I came back that night with a tattoo that said BERNHARD on my biceps. I acted like I didn't hear him. It was my first tattoo and everyone else was getting one so I got one, too. It was written in generic military block letters, because I couldn't think of anything else. Elmira had gotten "Bernhard" written in cursive so that it looked like "Love" upside down. I liked that, but I thought it would be weird if we'd both got the same one.

The next morning we all shuffled hungover to the cemetery where Bernhard was buried next to his father. Susan told me Bernhard's dad had never been around, but that, a year after Bernhard died, he felt so bad about it that he drank himself to death. He put in his will that he wanted to be buried next to his son, the war hero, and she had honored it. Elmira pulled out a bottle of Jameson and took a swig, said a few words about Bernhard, then passed it down the line, each of the guys repeating the pattern on down the line. Lieutenant Anderson hadn't been able to make it in person that year but said a few words over speakerphone when his turn came. I told the group that I felt guilty for filming what happened, and guilty just for being there, really.

Susan gave me a Native American blanket that she'd sewn. It was bright blue and had lots of cool shapes on it. I said I hoped releasing the movie was the right thing to do. She said it was. People would see how brave her son was. I agreed, even though I didn't think that's what people were going to take away from watching it. Whatever I hoped she'd get from the movie didn't matter; she was entitled to her feelings either way. Her youngest son was turning eighteen that year and was getting ready to join the Army. She said the Marines had refused him, out of respect for his brother.

I left the memorial a day before anyone else did. It was making me dizzy being around them all at once.

CHAPTER 15

Learned It from Them

I t always kind of surprised me that Dave Lillet, an old Marine buddy I went to Columbia with, hadn't become an extremist himself. On paper, Dave was a perfect candidate for it: strong-willed, hyperactive, constantly in need of some kind of purpose to pour all of his energy into. His GI Bill–funded excursion to a liberal arts college kind of saved him, like it had a lot of us. Sure, offering full tuition to every vet smart enough not to get in too much trouble cost a lot of taxpayer money, but you had to consider the alternative. Better to send us somewhere remote and peaceful after the military rather than watch a bunch of angry, young, combat-trained veterans get radicalized in the void of returning to civilian life. That's the idea, at least.

Now Dave had been recast as a newspaper reporter in Appalachia who spent his free time tracking and picking fights with veterans who had fallen into extremism. War was easy; all we had to do was not die. But that us-versus-them mentality that had been drilled into us from day one of basic training merged perfectly into the culture war that picked up after we returned home in the second decade of the twenty-first century. Dave was out there reporting on the January 6, 2021, riot. He told me he thought he'd seen guys from my former unit there with First Battalion, Sixth Marine Regiment patches on their flak jackets, news I found surprising but also unsurprising. I couldn't place any of them. "You remember Leman?" someone would ask me. "Maybe?" "Well, I think he was there." Pictures of guys all tac'd-up—covered in flak jackets and helmets and all the rest. It was hard to tell anymore; we all kind of looked the same. I could have sworn I ran into the Thousand Oaks, California, shooter somewhere in Helmand when I saw pics of him after the massacre. The jawline, the same haircut, the body primed in replicant form by Marine Corps physical fitness standards, us all-American corn-fed killers gone rotten and decrepit. GUNMAN WENT FROM MARINE TO LIVING WITH MOM, the headlines read.

Dave said there were so many vets in DC that day it was hard to tell them apart. Vets from Vietnam, vets from the Gulf War, vets from the Iraq War, vets who hadn't had a war of their own to screw up. Shit, even the dude wearing horns on his head had apparently been in the Navy at some point. It was like a modded-out *Call of Duty* level where soccer moms and small business owners became insurgents, a Veterans Day parade on methamphetamines, and the cameras attached at shoulder level to help them breach their target in style.

"You don't have January Sixth without GWOT," Dave told me (an acronym he insisted on pronouncing "gee-watt," for the Global War on Terror). "The Taliban haven't won the war militarily," Dave told me. "They're winning it politically here in the States. And we fucking learned from them. Why do you think the Proud Boys and Oath Keepers go recruiting so many vets? It's not just because of the clout that comes from having us in their ranks, it's because we know how to make fucking bombs, dude."

I knew in my heart that a lot of what happened there had to do with the cameras. And not just people wanting to be seen, or heard, like when we were out there in Helmand with our guns—tourists with guns—but with having seen too much. The filming, the constant recording (and thus *watching*) of everything from the reaches of outer space, to the aliens living in the deepest parts of the ocean, to our cringey social outbursts, to our internal organs, and soon to our souls—I knew that the filming and seeing had deprived us of a sense of reality for too long, of a curiosity for what life might bear in real time, and the goodness we gave each other the benefit of the doubt on. We were bloated from seeing. We'd been overexposed to the world and ourselves. You don't get flat-earth conspiracy theorists without the ability to see a livestream satellite view of earth on your phone or computer at any time. If you listened to the really crazy ones (as I often did), you start to hear a recurring theme: consciousness supposedly being suppressed by those in power.

"One thing, though," I said. "I'm not sure about your use of the word *insurgency*."

"Oh, dude, you have no idea how bad it's gotten. I'm tracking these motherfuckers. They're everywhere. The FBI now considers them one of the top threats to national security."

As much as I liked the idea of White supremacists being targeted the same way Muslims had been for the past twenty years, it didn't seem very productive. It felt like this was the American way: get extremely worked up over something, then demonize the group responsible, then slowly pull back to try to understand where the roots of the problem were coming from, only to realize that it was too late and the problem had become normalized, then get bludgeoned by another problem that was taking the old one's place.

"I guess I'm just a little fearful of otherizing each other. Like, I'm not minimizing what these people did or what they stand for. . . ."

"Dude."

"What?"

"You didn't see the way they were."

" . . . "

"They were literally frothing at the mouth. I was right there next to them while they were bear-spraying cops and smashing in windows."

I could see where this was going. "You're gonna say it, aren't you?" I asked.

"What?"

"You're gonna fucking say it. Go ahead."

"What??"

"That I wasn't there, so I don't know."

"Well . . . you weren't, dude."

When the Taliban inevitably took back power, the withdrawal felt oddly in sync with January 6th. Both a complete and total shit show. Maybe Dave was right, maybe it was all GWOT coming home. And just like with January 6th, which some people were blaming on Antifa, there were people who actually thought that the Afghans in the video running and holding on to the engine of the C-130 were crisis actors. But even scarier and stupider and more alarming, CNN was acting like we desperately needed another troop surge to go reclaim Kabul. *You dumb drum-beating motherfuckers*, I thought. *You corporate hogs*. Did they not realize that the Afghan Army had been getting slaughtered for the past six years (without pay, mind you) since we'd stopped patrolling with them? Did they not understand that the only thing keeping Kabul from being overrun was our air support, and that the Afghan soldiers who had been getting slaughtered and having their families slaughtered were no longer interested in dying for a country that was not really a country? That the majority of Afghans were farmers who didn't want their families and houses being bombed anymore for the sake of a few barely propped-up democracies in Herat and Kabul?

It was especially hard when I finally got ahold of Wahid; old, jaded Wahid. He had been calling senators, Marine officers he'd served with, embassies, anyone who could help him get his family out of Afghanistan. They were on the run; the Taliban knew about his work with us and were leaving them death threats. They were there at Kabul Airport when the bomb went off that took out 180 people, a few of whom were Marines who were born after 9/11—the news kept emphasizing that, as if the war had still been about 9/11 when we millennials were there. When his family tried to make a run for Pakistan, they were denied entry, and eventually they had to go into hiding because his mom had a stroke from all the stress.

Wahid had been one of the most anti-Muslim Muslims I'd ever met when we were in Afghanistan together. He ate pork in front of the other terps, much to their chagrin, and openly derided the prophet Muhammad. Now, he told me, he had started praying again for the first time since he was kid. Back before he was "corrupted by the Marines."

When he texted me that he'd given up and that the U.S. had abandoned his family, I didn't know what to say. Although I wanted to comfort him, part of me also wanted to say he should have seen this coming. In fact, I knew he'd seen it coming because we'd been talking about it for the past five years.

This is what we do, dude. It's what America does best, I texted him back.

I wasn't trying to sound callous, but either out of contempt or just not wanting to hear my shit right then, he blocked me. And I saw that we had not only fucked yet another Middle Eastern/West Asian country, but I might have lost a friend, and not just a friend, but an idea of friendship that I wasn't sure I believed in anymore.

I started going on death binges on the internet. I know I'm not unique in doing this. It happens after being so sucked dry that you start needing a pick-me-up to give your life some substance. But the death videos don't wake you up; they may give you nightmares for a couple of days, but they don't wake you up. They make you feel less alive, like murder was a construct. I watched the Rittenhouse video and didn't sleep well for a night. However, it wasn't because of the horror of the real; it was because of the way the video was shot, the way the man recording couldn't stop recording, even after Rittenhouse had gotten up and ran away. It was the man's breathing, which intensified after he'd walked a safe distance away and the realization of what had happened came pouring over him.

I couldn't help but feel I had some responsibility for all of it, that the propaganda videos I'd made for the Marine Corps weren't all that different from the ones recruiting young men into the far right. That even *Combat Obscura* would end up getting kids to enlist or do some other crazy shit, because it was real and dirty and wasn't what the military wanted you to see and we were in a post-factual world where everything was in the eye of the beholder. I had devoted most of my life after getting out of the military-industrial complex to making something that would scare the fuck out of kids like me, to prevent them from making the same mistake. But the stats didn't lie: one of the most popular destinations for viewing my documentary was on Xbox, where, presumably, kids were taking a break from *Battlefield* and *Call of Duty* to get a dose of "real war," to feed the need for real gore and merge the two together in perfect harmony—the fake and the real. What happens when they become indistinguishable from each other?

I went on Letterboxd.com and saw a kid had posted a review of *Combat Obscura*:

"HAHAHA YOU LOST BITCH GO TO HELL. BURN THERE. damn didnt they teach you how to use a camera in propaganda school? not even the basics of exposure or composition? Rough." Posted by Kyle.

Damn you, Kyle. It wasn't enough to taunt me for losing the war? You also had to critique my camera work?

———

It made you want to drink, the precariousness of it all. The VA was worried enough about its vets to send "don't kill yourself" postcards in the mail. My wife and I had split up and I was rooming with a sixty-year-old gay masseur named Damerae, whom I'd met on Craigslist. We'd get coked and molly'd up and watch movies and YouTube videos all night, and he'd tell me about New York in the eighties, how much realer it was. And that was the problem, he said: everyone was trying to be real these days but it was really, really hard now. I felt my high school self looking down on me. And I was watching trash TV for what felt like twenty-four hours a day. Getting soft. Damerae told me I should take it easy.

One night I did the corniest thing I've ever done in my life. I had been up all night working my way through a twelve-pack, gobbling psilocybin mushrooms like they were cashews and feeling guilty for things I hadn't done yet. Damerae had barricaded himself in his room because I had kept trying to get in and talk to him.

"Hey, Dam. Gotta talk to ya, bud," I said, rapping at his door.

"*No*. I'm sleeping. I didn't sign up for this, dude," he responded. I tried to bust through the door but he had done a real good job of keeping it shut. Then I wandered back into the living room and watched *Eyes Wide Shut* for the seven hundredth time, and the coded messages came shining through, thanks to the mushrooms. Then I watched *Avatar*, which I now saw wasn't such a bad movie. I get it; it's fun, like a roller coaster. Seriously, no hard feelings.

Eventually I called the veterans' crisis line and told the lady on the phone that I had executed someone in Afghanistan.

"He was wounded, and we just killed him," I said.

"Oh no, honey, I'm so sorry," she said.

"You're sorry for me? What about the guy I killed?"

"War makes us do things that we would never normally do."

"So, we should get a pass?" I asked.

She took a moment to think about this. "You don't get a pass, but hoarding the guilt isn't going to help anyone. You have to process the memories, not keep reliving them." I could tell by her voice that she was an older Black lady whose father had been in Vietnam. She sounded passionate, but I wondered how many calls like this she'd already taken that night.

During the past few months, it had gotten harder and harder for me to determine whether what I had in my head was real or not. I had started losing the glue even further since moving out of my wife's place. She and I were the same person, you see. Not personality-wise, but in our bones. Her smell was my smell. When I looked at photos of her, I couldn't help seeing myself in her face, and when I looked in the mirror she was there, too, like our genetic code had merged, or like one of those face-mix apps on people's phones.

I took a pause from the veteran's crisis call to text Ciara about the man we'd executed, just in case she'd assumed that I was doing well post-breakup.

"Have you consumed anything tonight, honey?" the crisis lady asked.

"Just beer," I lied.

"No pills or anything? I just ask because you sound a bit groggy."

"No."

Soon she called the cops and they came and carted me off, and I felt I was getting the celebrity treatment. Cops in New York have a hard-on for veterans, especially young White ones. We were still fresh souls to be saved, to bond with over their presumed idea of a shared identity. The call to service that elevates us from the rest of the herd, or some such bullshit. They put a shirt on me and patted me on the back, and I felt the love like an invalid elephant man being caressed for the first time.

"My nephew was in Iraq," one of them said. "I know what you all have been through. You made the right decision to call the crisis line, Jacob."

"It's Miles," I said.

———

At the hospital they put me in a pen with some other loonies and wished me luck. No one was tending to them except for an old Jamaican lady sitting in the hallway who kept yelling at everyone to be quiet and keep their masks on. There was a scary redheaded woman who was writhing around in bed making contorted faces at me like a silent film star. I brought her some water, but then all the others wanted some, too, and I began handing little cups out to each of them. They showered me with thanks and looked at me like I was Mother Teresa, except for this crusty old drunk who knew I was full of shit.

"You're not on TV," he kept telling me. "There ain't no cameras here." Old drunks are always trying to make you feel insecure. They get off on it.

A doctor with a clipboard came in and asked me if I was still thinking about hurting myself. I told him I wasn't and that I'd only called the crisis line because my roommate wouldn't talk to me. He told me they'd have to admit me into their psych ward for at least a few days, then he left. Eventually I got sick of refilling everyone's water cups and decided I'd leave, too. Before I did, I turned to the old drunk and told him he was wrong. I pointed to a security camera on the ceiling, and we both busted up laughing like it was the wittiest goddamn thing either of us had ever heard. I felt like Jesus's son as I walked out of the place past the Jamaican woman, who said tepidly, without looking up from her phone, that I couldn't leave yet.

When I got out on the street, I checked my texts. Ciara had responded: "You already told me you weren't there when they killed him. And if you keep texting me I'm going to block you."

I decided to ignore this negative energy. I felt alive and filled with the curiosity of a newborn cat. I was so curious that I wound up in Highbridge Park, a junkie fantasia in Washington Heights, to see if I could score something fresh that would keep this feeling going. It was there that I ran into Louis Sanon, an overweight, oversensitive old high school friend-turned-writer-turned-junkie. He'd lost a scholarship to Brown because of it. When we were kids, he used to follow me home from school because we'd both been pretending to read *Naked Lunch* our junior year.

When I caught his eye, he nearly fell off the rock he was sitting on. He told me he'd been waiting for me. I said he was full of shit. I told him he fell too hard for anyone who inspired the least bit of connection. One of our English teachers had had to remove him from our class because he kept sending her creepy emails.

"That's why I love you, man," he said with a lazy, dopesick grin. "You always keep it real."

It didn't matter. I was going to shoot heroin for the first time and that would be something. Louis kept missing my veins in the dark and I cursed him each time. I said I thought he was supposed to be good at this, which he took very personally. I shined my phone flashlight and tried to hold the bandages that were dripping with blood at the same time, and eventually he got it in.

I stood up and felt so young again. I was walking on air through used syringes, K-2 bags, and condoms. I felt a shimmering joy in my chest that warned me I might die if I stopped moving.

I asked him why I felt so up when heroin was supposed to be down.

"I would never give you H, Miles. I care too much about you."

This really pissed me off. "I wanted to try heroin," I said. It was more cinematic. I once dated a girl, a "filmmaker," who said her sole ambition in life was to become rich and famous enough that she could try heroin safely. The millennial artist's embryonic dream. Lou, himself, had pretty much admitted he'd become a junkie because he listened to too much Amy Winehouse in high school, back when we would sneak into repossessed tenements in Tribeca and drink cheap liquor and play weird mind games with each other.

I was a fly caught in his trap as he tried to sit me down and talk about what had happened way back then.

"Why did you first talk to me?" he asked. "And why did you join the Army?"

"Marines," I corrected him. "And you talked to me first."

I wanted to go run with the bulls, not sit here and reminisce. There was something unnerving about the intensity of his nostalgia.

"Do you realize how long it's been since we've seen each other? This is a sign."

"Mm," I said. I had been getting a lot of signs lately. Signs that I was not a very good person, even after all the years since getting out of the Marines, years I was supposed to be devoting to becoming a better person, but had failed at.

"You know, when you left you didn't even say good-bye," he said. "You didn't call me for five years. That was the hardest part."

My heart sank and then opened up again as I remembered our last day of school together before I enlisted, me scaling along the ledge of the five-story building that looked like a prison but was our high school, from one classroom in through the window to Ms. Linn's journalism class, and her screaming, "YOU FUCKING ASSHOLE! YOU FUCKING ASSHOLE! GET THE FUCK OFF OF THERE! GET THE FUCK OUT OF HERE!" and Louis sitting there shaking his head at me like I was scum. It was the way he was looking at me that made me decide I would cut ties with him forever. But also, I wanted his last image of me to be on that ledge.

"Have I changed?" he asked suddenly. "Be honest."

It was an absurd question. He was virtually unrecognizable, both physically and mentally. Old needle scars reopened and then scarred over again, track marks running from the backs of his hands up his arms; black, soulless eyes that used to be filled with youthful wonder; fidgety, unstable emotions that had taken the place of genuine confidence and intellect. He used to be sharp as fuck; maybe too sharp. But I lied and told him he was still the same person underneath it all. There was still a Louis somewhere in there.

The sun was coming up and we began to walk, so Louis could score some more and we could keep talking, and I realized the secret of success: to be awake and holy during these earthly, untouchable hours.

"When everything feels like small talk, and the homeless lose their mystique and become nothing more than nuisances, then you've lost the game," he said. "We used to say that, remember?"

"I always thought I would be the one who'd end up on the streets," I said. "I guess you beat me to it."

EPILOGUE

Elmira told me when he's feeling really fucked up, he goes into his basement, away from the wife and kids, and plays *Combat Obscura*, but just the sound—turning up the volume during the part where Bernhard gets shot—till it's reverberating off his walls and consumes him.

"Whoosah," he tells me. The sound brings him a sense of being whole again. "You ever press down on a cut or bruise?" he asked. The wounds we've created for ourselves having to be poked and prodded to remind us of where our lives got derailed. In that moment, it almost makes everything going wrong in the country recede for a second. It resets him. All the things he was afraid of: the "woke colleges" that his sons were about to go to, the misinformation, the cancel culture, the "race card," the vaccines and how everyone was blindly going along with everything, some references to the Bible and numbers I didn't quite catch.

"The Marine Corps was a melting pot," he said. "Sure, we were still cliqued up by race, but it was the kinda thing where, you take me home to your fam, I'll take you home to mine." He told me he'd gone over to Doc Coleman's family's place for dinner once, and learned about how his dad had been taken out of school when he was a kid because of segregation. That was something he apparently had to learn about from the source.

"But now we're just doin' the same thing," he said, sighing heavily. "In my southern mind, I try to make sense of it, but . . . you gotta meet me halfway."

I went out to see Loya in El Paso. This time because *he* was worried about *me* (I had been texting him too the night the cops took me to the hospital). But I had been doing better. Not as good as him, but getting there (I'd successfully avoided getting blocked by my wife, and we were patching things up sort of). He was pretty squared away now, working on the railroads that ran through New Mexico and Texas, resetting the tracks when they got skewed, and he was engaged to a woman with a thirteen-year-old kid. He was always dating women with kids; we used to say he had Jerry Maguire syndrome because he fell for the kids more than the women. His fiancée didn't speak English. She was from Juarez, and she had a real sleezy stoner laugh even though she didn't smoke weed. Her daughter was cute and funny as hell. They were a happy family.

Loya took me dove hunting in the desert. We drove out into the middle of two freeways and shot a bunch of doves. When we went to Walmart so I could get my hunting license, they said that was the only game in season, and so we said fuck it, kind of laughing about it, killing the international bird of peace just as the war was coming to an end (for *us* at least). But it was fucked up because the way to distinguish the doves from the pigeons was that the doves sort of made the symbol for international peace when they came swooping into the clearing—with wings out and head up like a Nike swoosh, imaginary olive branch in their mouth—and that's when you'd know it was a dove and you'd take the shot.

As we sat by a little stream they used for water, waiting for another batch of them to come flying in, Loya told me he was sorry for leaving me to work on the footage all alone. He said it was a fucked-up thing to do, and that he was proud of me for finishing it, and he was proud to have his name in the cinematography credits as well.

"I love you, bro," he said, as if I needed that. Which I did.

Sometimes, even if you lose your faith in humanity, you can still have faith in a certain person, whether because of their goodness, or loyalty, or whatever. That was Loya for me.

We must have killed over thirty doves that day, his friend Pablo and I; Loya couldn't hit anything. Every time he'd miss, Pablo, who looked like a Mexican militia member in the woodland fatigues and bandana he was wearing, would call him a bitch.

"You sure you were in the Marines, bro?" he'd say, laughing as he blasted his shotgun into the air, taking out three consecutive doves in a row. Loya just smiled. When Pablo went off to go draw more of them out, Loya turned to me and asked me bluntly about the man we executed.

"Were you there when they killed the dude or not?" he asked.

"I don't know, you know? I think a part of me needed to be there . . ." I said.

Loya just nodded. He could understand anything you confessed, even if what you were saying didn't make a whole lot of sense.

"The life of the mind," he said, as he missed another dove that came swooping into the clearing. I took it out after it did some lizard-brained evasive maneuver that brought it back into my line of fire. I didn't feel bad about all the bird killing till we had to rip their breast meat out, and I could see all the little bird feed they'd been eating that day. For some reason that made me unbearably sad. I always get sad thinking about animals and people eating.

Loya kept disappearing to go collect the dead ones. We were

going to make jalapeño poppers with the bits of breast meat later. He said we should put the meat inside the jalapeños and add cream cheese, anything really to take away from the taste of the dove meat, which was apparently not very good. But at least this killing wouldn't go to waste.

It was after the fifth time he disappeared that I decided to go walk around a bit, past the trees surrounded by shotgun shells, and rocks graffitied by other generations of Loya-like kids. I imagined him as a youth, running around these same parts, chasing after life before it had beaten us all down, before his second wind came. He was in his second wind now; I could see that for sure. I remembered when he stayed with me in New York after we'd gotten out, how exhausted and dead to the world he seemed. But now he was fresh again. And even if the second wind wasn't as intense or interesting as the first, it was still something. It had opened a world inside him that allowed new things to come in without the drag of comparing it to the past.

"I think we peaked in Afghanistan," Dave from the riot told me once, when we were at Columbia.

Psh. Not Loya. He was still peaking.

I came over a sandy hill and saw him beneath me in a clearing, huddled over a dove I'd shot that was still alive, spasming out. Gently, he picked it up and broke its neck with a quick twist, then with both hands put it, sort of decorously, into the dump pouch he had on his side. Then he moved on to the next one, protecting me from my own sins. Apparently, a lot of the ones I'd shot weren't dead yet. I was leading them too much, maybe, or not enough. Still not getting the kill shot.

On the drive back to Loya's place, I wondered when my second wind would come, if ever. I made a list of things I would have to do: would have to call Wahid if he wasn't still blocking me, see how his mom was doing. Would have to call my mom, see how she was doing. Would have to get sober like Loya, stop fucking around. Would have to finish writing this book before I went insane.

As we drove through the red, ugly desert that kept expanding and crushing the inner lives of all its people, I felt like we'd be swallowed up into something else. And Loya kept his eyes on the road.

ACKNOWLEDGMENTS

I want to thank everyone who pushed me to write this thing when I didn't think I had anything new to say about the war: Kirby Kim, Eloy Bleifuss, and the Janklow crew. Thanks also to Loren, Chris, and Sean for opening me up to a voice I didn't know I had.

Thank you, Nick Ciani, my editor, and everyone at One Signal who helped shape this book.

Thanks to all my film professors for keeping the faith alive.

To lifelong friends: Desmond, Pete, Eric the Schumanator, Iris, Gleb, Alex, Kyle, Justin, Sammy G., Rory, Allison, Nasim, and Abby. And to those who didn't make it.

Thank you to my mom and dad, and sorry for joining the Marines. I promise I won't do it again.

Finally, thanks to my wife, Ciara, for taking me back and saving my life, even when I didn't deserve it.

In loving memory of Marge, AKA, G.

INDEX

ABOUT THE AUTHOR

Miles Lagoze is the director of the critically acclaimed 2019 documentary *Combat Obscura*. The footage used in the documentary was obtained when Lagoze enlisted as an eighteen-year-old Combat Camera in the Marines and deployed to Afghanistan in 2011. His writing has been published by *The Paris Review* and *RealClearPolitics*. *Whistles from the Graveyard* is his first book.